WOR G

WOR GEORDIE

GEORGE HARBRON

First published by Shakspeare Editorial, May 2021

ISBN pbk 978-1-9993295-7-0
ISBN ebk 978-1-9993295-8-7

Design and typesetting www.ShakspeareEditorial.org

Photographs © G.T. Harbron

Dedicated to my mother for her love and care

Kids from Kirton Street, Railway Terrace

With thanks to Sister Tate

Chapter 1

H E WAS ONLY a young lad, eight years of age, living in the North East of England, in a one-bedroom, upstairs flat with his seven brothers and sisters.

Dad was a pitman, working underground. His job, as it was known at the time, was a stone-man. A hard, brutal job, but people took this type of work on for the money. Before that, Dad had been in the army for the duration of the Second World War. He'd told them one of the places they'd sent him to had been Africa, where he had caught malaria; other than that, he very rarely talked about it.

Geordie's Mam kept house, looking after everyone, making sure there was always plenty on the table, getting them off to school looking as tidy as she could get them.

The one-bedroom flat had a small kitchen and a toilet outside, down the back stairs to a small backyard that led out into the back lane. The yard was shared with the downstairs neighbour. The toilets were separated by a four-inch brick wall. If they were occupied at the same time people could have a conversation with each other, which happened often – especially between kids! The yard also contained two small coalhouses that were kept well away from each other as, if one was full of coal and the other was empty, it was far too much of a temptation to loosen a brick and help yourself to your neighbour's coal – especially on a cold winter night.

Things were not easy in 1947 (far from it) but people made the best of what they had back then. But if your dad was a pitman who received a ton of coal every month, courtesy of the National Coal Board, you had a good commodity. Mam would always sell some to her neighbours. When it was delivered they tipped it in the back lane for Mam to shovel into two large galvanised tin buckets. She wouldn't trust anyone to do it for her as you could guarantee some of it would go missing. Either Geordie or his older sister was always told to watch the coal in the back lane, while Mam carried it into the coalhouse.

Geordie was no different from any other kid running around in the cobbled streets and back lanes of Gateshead and Newcastle on Tyneside. But trouble always seemed to follow him around, no matter what he did. Many were the times when, after a loud knock on his front door, their neighbours would stand watching, whispering and talking.

'There's a copper at number five again.'

'Oh, aye and you know who that will be for don't you?'

'It'll be for that young Geordie of hers. What a life she's got with him.'

Geordie was constantly in trouble one way or another – it always seemed to be him who ended up getting caught. It was nothing big time, he was too young for that. Nevertheless, it was the things that parents could well do without, like minor brushes with the law after stealing bits and pieces from shops. Geordie and his little mob were banned from the bigger shops on the High Street, like Woolworths and Littlewoods.

Many's the time they trespassed on the railway lines if they could find nothing else to occupy themselves. There was a seven-foot stone wall separating the houses from the railway that they had no problem climbing over. What they couldn't get into their heads was that it was a dangerous place to be, with trains running past every fifteen minutes or so. Plus the fact that some of the lines were live; step on them and you would fry like an egg. Nine times out of ten they were seen and chased by railway workers. Only once were they ever caught, but just given a warning and thrown off the railway land.

~

One weekday when the schools were on holiday, and with nothing else to do, three of them left the small park at the top of their street (if it could be called a park, with its three swings and a roundabout that caused more injuries than it was worth).

They headed off toward the High Street with nothing particular in mind. There was one entrance that had a partition in the middle of it to form two shops. On one side of the partition they sold clothes and on the other side they sold chocolates and sweets. This proved very tempting for the three of them. One stayed near the entrance and if anyone came in they would start coughing very loudly. Geordie went behind the counter and stuffed his pockets with sweets, while his mate kept an eye out for the person who served coming back into their side of the shop.

Before they knew it, the shop assistant came back from the other side of the partition. His mate ran like hell out the entrance, leaving Geordie under the counter. The owner came rushing around from the other side on hearing the commotion, and caught Geordie under the counter. He told the assistant to close the door in case he made a dash for it. As usual, Geordie gave a false name and address. They called for a policeman. The main police station was only a few hundred yards away, at the bottom of the High Street. Before long, an elderly policeman walked into the shop, where he found Geordie sitting in a chair. While the officer was asking where he lived, Geordie's mate came walking into the shop, as brazen as brass.

'Oh, I know him; he's Charley Dodds,' he said, looking at the officer.

'Is he now?' replied the officer. 'Listen young man, you go and tell his mam where he is and that I want to speak to her. If you don't do it quick I'm going to arrest you instead of him. Now go.'

His mate turned on his heels and ran as fast as his legs could carry him.

The next thing he knew, his Mam was walking into the shop, still wearing her pinny and turban with a coat on top. The officer told the shop owner that they might have a job to prosecute owing to Geordie's age, and that a caution would most likely do the trick and give him a fright so he'd not do it again. His Mam apologised to the shop owner and told him she'd make sure that he never stepped into his shop again. She was relieved to hear the owner agreeing with the officer. They left the shop with his Mam holding him by the scruff of his neck.

She gave him a hard shake, saying, 'I'll bloody well kill you when we get home.'

Mam didn't lay a finger on him, but she did tell his Dad what had happened. He wanted to give him a good hiding, but his Mam managed to persuade him not to, much to Geordie's relief.

~

Things settled down, but it didn't take long before he and his little mob, having nothing else to do, decided they would head for the High Street again. As they approached the local cinema, Old Blacks, they decided they'd try and gain entrance through one of the side doors, which they'd done on so many occasions. They were unable to open the first door, the steel proved to be too much for them. Someone suggested trying the doors on the other side of the building, up an alleyway. While they were quietly trying to prise one open, they heard a commotion at the alley entrance. Two men were arguing and they could see that both of them were drunk. That put a stop to what they were up to. One of the drunks decided he'd had enough and started walking away. Geordie and his mates did their best to get past them. Then the unthinkable happened. The drunk still in the alleyway shouted and swore, took his last drink from his bottle, then threw it at the other drunk. The bottle flew through the air and hit Geordie on the back of his head. He kept on running until they were on the main footpath, but a few minutes later Geordie fell to his knees. He was dizzy and his mates' voices were echoing as he heard one of them saying he'd seen him get hit with a beer bottle.

They headed back home with him. By the time they got to their back lane Geordie had pulled himself around. He was still a bit dizzy but didn't want to get in trouble with his Mam or Dad, so he sat in his backyard until he felt a bit better and went up the back stairs to get his tea. He didn't tell his Mam what had happened, he simply told her that he didn't feel well.

Mam felt his brow, 'Well, you haven't got a temperature but get yourself to bed, you might be coming down with something. We'll see what you're like in the morning.'

He didn't argue, he was just pleased to go to sleep. Even when his brothers crawled into the bed, he didn't wake up. There were three beds squeezed into the one small room: one for his Mam and Dad, one for his sisters, and one for him and his brothers.

On the Monday, when he had to go back to school, he
told his Mam that he didn't feel well. She felt his brow, but he
felt all right to her. He then told her he had a 'bad head', but
he had played that card once too often, so Mam wasn't having
any of it and chased him off to school.

At the school gates he met one of his mates who had been
with him in the alley, 'How's ya heed Geordie?'

'Aw, it's all reet. Still got a cut in it though, ind a still feel
a bit sick.'

'Did yi tell ya mam what happened?'

'Nah, a git in enough trouble to start with with oot looking
for it.'

'If yi still feel sick why divint we dee a bunk from school
then?'

'Nah, not the day. A just want ti sit doon, me heed's killing
is.'

'Yi should have gittin ya mam to put a plaster on that
head of yors.'

'Aw shut up will yi. I've got a bad head with oot yea
ganning on.'

In the school playground the noise from all the kids
shouting wasn't helping Geordie's headache one little bit. He
knew that something was wrong, he was getting sensations in
the top of his legs, and his arms, and was glad when the bell
went for them all to go to their classrooms.

He sat at his desk as the forty or more kids took not the
slightest notice of the teacher. The teacher never bothered you
unless you were talking or messing about, disturbing what he
was trying to teach. It was a change to find Geordie so quiet
in class as he was usually the instigator of any disturbance.

Halfway through the lesson Geordie again felt the
sensations in his thighs and at the top of his arms. Something
was wrong and it was beginning to frighten him. The room

started to spin and the teacher's voice echoed in his head. He closed his eyes tightly and everything went blank. Half the class got the fright of their lives as Geordie shook the life out of his desk, causing it to bounce all over the place.

The teacher quickly sent a child to fetch the headmaster, Mr. May, 'And tell him its urgent,' he shouted after him.

The headmaster came rushing into the classroom as Geordie was coming around. The teacher had placed him on the floor. On opening his eyes, he saw the teacher and the headmaster leaning over him and straight away he started to blabber.

'It wasn't my fault sir. It wasn't my fault. I didn't mean to do anything, honest.'

Mr May calmed him down, told him he'd done nothing wrong and took him to his office, telling him that he was not well. In the meantime, he instructed the teacher to send someone who knew where he lived to inform his Mam that the headmaster needed to see her urgently.

Sunderland Road School was only a few minutes' walk from where they lived so it wasn't long before Geordie's Mam came hurrying through the school gates. She knew it would be about Geordie, as her other kids rarely got into bother. She wondered what the hell he could have done now as she knocked on the headmaster's door. She was right, there was Geordie sitting in the corner of the office. Mam felt angrier than she'd been for a while as she asked the headmaster, 'What has he been up to now?'

Mr May asked her to take a seat and explained that he hadn't done anything wrong. That her son had been at his desk in the middle of a class when he suddenly took an epileptic fit. She was shocked, it had never happened to him before. The headmaster told her that he had noticed a small cut on the back of her son's head and some dried blood. He pointed this out so she wouldn't think that it had happened while he was at school.

Mr May was a tall slim man who towered over Geordie's Mam, he was also a kind man who never lost his temper or shouted at the kids in his school. He asked Mam if this had happened before. She replied that this was the first time as far as she knew. She walked across to Geordie to look at the back of his head and asked him how it had happened. She also noticed a small indent surrounding the cut. The headmaster suggested that she take him to see her doctor or to the hospital casualty department. Mam thanked him and took Geordie home first, then to see the family doctor later that day.

Once they were home Mam started to question him about what had happened before he had taken the fit. Geordie told her that he had felt funny and started getting funny feelings in his legs and arms and that things didn't look right to him. When she asked him what he meant by that, he couldn't explain. She asked him how he had cut his head, so he told her about the two drunks and how one of them had thrown the beer bottle that hit his head.

'And did you blank out after it happened?' she asked.

'No, but I felt dizzy and a bit sick. I wasn't sick Mam, but I felt funny and tired.'

'Right,' she said after she had bathed the back of his head. 'Get your coat on, I'm taking you to the doctor's.'

Mam told the doctor what had happened, from when the hurt occurred to what had happened at school. After the doctor inspected the back of Geordie's head, he told Mam that it was probably concussion and he wanted her to take Geordie to the Q-E Hospital for a check-up. He also told her not to worry, as it could be just a one-off.

Mam took Geordie straight to the hospital. After a long wait, they were seen and told that they could see the small indent where the cut was but that they could see no serious damage to the head itself. They also confirmed what the family doctor had told them, and that he had a slight concussion, telling Mam to keep an eye on him for the next few days. The family doctor had told Mam to fetch him back in one week for a check-up. Mam left the hospital, still worrying herself over him.

Geordie was kept off school for a few weeks so his Mam could keep an eye on him. It was hard for her to do that and do everything else around the house. What with washing Dad's pit clothes and the rest of the family's clothes, plus getting dinners and teas ready for everyone.

~

Not being at school suited Geordie fine as he had a mate next door who missed a lot of schooling because he suffered from asthma. He was younger than Geordie by a couple of years, but when they got together they could cause their mams a right headache.

Three days into the first week off school Geordie took a fit in the middle of the night, which woke the whole household. Mam wasn't sure what to do about it, other than to hold him in her arms, telling the others it was 'all right'. It stopped in just over a minute, when Geordie lay still and fell back to sleep.

Mam sat in the kitchen with a cup of tea. Her mind was turning things over and over, worrying about what might happen to him. Worrying that if he took a fit and she wasn't there he could get seriously hurt. All kinds of images ran through her head, as she knew fine well that he could be a handful at the best of times.

The following morning she got the rest of the kids off to school, left the youngest one with the next-door neighbour, and took Geordie to the family doctor.

He asked Mam about what she'd done when he took a fit, how long was he in it, did he fall asleep straight after or later on? After that he asked Geordie to try and explain how he felt before he took his fit and what he felt like when he came out of it, plus other questions Geordie didn't quite understand.

When he was finished the doctor wrote out a prescription, telling Mam they were anti-convulsion capsules and were to be taken three times a day. He told her to come back again in one week to see how Geordie had progressed.

Mam went straight to the chemist, only to be told by the assistant she had to pay for them. The label on the bottle said it was Epanutin, to be taken three times a day – as the doctor had prescribed. Back home Mam took out one of the capsules, not sure how to give it to Geordie. She cut out a piece of newspaper, opened the capsule and poured out the powder on to the newspaper, like taking Beechhams powders. She told Geordie to open his mouth and put out his tongue, she put the powder on his tongue and told him to drink water from a cup. The powder tasted extremely bitter, he didn't like it at all. Mam told him he had better get used to it as he had to take it three times every day to make him well.

'But I'm not bad, Mam.'

'You don't realise it son, but yes, you are.'

CHAPTER 2

As THE WEEKS went by his condition slowly got worse. Geordie was taking about three fits a week, on a good week only two. Sometimes he took one at night in his sleep, when his Mam would sit holding him until he went back to sleep. Problem was, she couldn't watch him twenty-four hours a day, as much as she would have wanted to.

His mates were getting used to seeing him looking like he was fighting with himself on the ground. He was lucky that the fits lasted for less than two minutes and he was back on his feet, although at times he was groggy and slightly dizzy. He was supposed to tell his Mam whenever he had taken one, but half the time he didn't mention it to her. She only found out when one of his mates mentioned it in front of her. He was back to his old self as far as getting into trouble.

He had been on his medication for some six months and nothing had improved. It was one of those Saturday's when they were bored stiff, when the next small chapter in Geordie's life came along. They had tried to get into the school playground to have a kick about with their ball, but the grounds were well secured and locked up, plus the caretaker was hanging around.

They strolled along the main road, up to any trouble they could find. One of them noticed the small top window above the entrance to one of the stores was open. They couldn't see anyone inside, and they all thought the shop was shut. But everyone was in a room at the back having their dinner break.

Geordie, as the best climber, went through first, then his mate, leaving the the third outside to keep an eye out – not that he'd be able to do anything about it if somebody came to open the store. While they were rummaging around under the counter someone appeared from out of nowhere. His mate made a dash for the small window, with Geordie hot on his heels. Neither of them realised that they could have opened the door simply by turning the latch. His mate was that slow trying to get out that the person could grab Geordie's feet. His two mates ran like hell, leaving Geordie held by the scruff of his neck once again.

He was taken to the police station, where the manager said he had no choice but to press charges against him, regardless of his age. His Mam was absolutely furious when she was asked to go down to the police station. When they told her the store was insisting on pressing charges, she was stunned.

When Mam got him home and told his Dad about it he hit the roof.

'I'll frigging show him what's right and wrong,' he shouted, taking off his broad belt.

Geordie dashed into the bedroom in fright as Dad started lashing out. The belt caught him as he crawled further under the beds. Mam heard him cry out and hurried into the bedroom, screaming at Dad as she grabbed at the belt.

'Here give me that, yi want to kill him? I'll kill him for yi.'

Mam lifted the nearest bed up on its side, mattress and all, and started lashing out at him, not that she actually caught him with the belt. But Dad didn't see that, he was off for a pint, he'd had enough for one night.

It wasn't his Dad or his belt that put the fear into Geordie, it was that his Mam was hitting him with it, and she looked that mad. It was the first time she had ever raised a hand to him.

All Geordie did for the next week was go to school, he was not even allowed to play in the back lane. Later in the week Mam received a letter from Gateshead police telling her that she and Geordie were to appear in front of the Magistrate's Court in Gateshead.

He overheard his Dad telling his Mam, 'That one's going to turn out to be a bad-un, I'm telling you woman, you mark my word for it.'

The week after that he was standing in a Juvenile Court in front of someone who looked like he was in charge, just like his school headmaster.

Mam thought the same as Dad, that he was too young for them to do much about him. Mam had looked in a dictionary to see what 'juvenile delinquency' meant, and believed it meant 'people below the age of legal responsibility', so she was thinking he would be all right and he'd probably end up getting a good telling off. Nevertheless, it was a frightening experience for both of them to be standing there in the courtroom.

The person who was doing most of the talking looked across at Mam, telling her that he was an intelligent young boy who knew right from wrong, and that a short spell in a remand home may make him think twice the next time he decided to do something which he should not be doing, and that it might change his ways. Geordie didn't have any idea what was going on. Even his Mam wasn't sure what was happening until someone explained that she couldn't take him home with her, and that he was to be sent to South Hetton Remand Home until further notice. Mam nearly collapsed when she heard this. She tried her best to tell them that her son was not well and was prone to taking fits and needed to take his medication. No one seemed to be interested in what she was trying to say.

Mam went straight to the doctor's from the court to explain what had happened. After a few phone calls he told her that Geordie would receive his medication that same afternoon. He said he'd tried his best to tell whoever was on the other end of the phone that in his professional opinion 'where they had placed him was not where he should be in his condition', and he wanted that to be known.

Mam went home, still in shock and not knowing what to tell the family or neighbours when they noticed he wasn't there.

~

South Hetton Remand Home was full of kids a lot older than Geordie. Halfway through the second week the people in charge had enough, and said they wouldn't take responsibility if anything happened to him. He was taking too many fits and they were not qualified to give him medication, never mind dealing with him when he was unconscious.

He was returned home and was glad to be back. He hadn't liked the place at all, everything was regimental: no talking; going to bed and getting up at the same times; meals at set times; and so on. Yes, Geordie was pleased to be home, playing once again in his own back lane.

The seizures happened more frequently. Mam was up at night after he'd taken one. He was disturbing the whole family.

The education department had informed Mam that they would not be held responsible if anything happened to him during a seizure as his teachers were neither equipped nor trained to handle such situations. Nevertheless, Geordie still had to be educated, same as any other kid in Gateshead. So, he continued to go to the school at the top of his street, as they had nowhere else they could send him.

CHAPTER 3

S UMMER OF 1948. School holidays had arrived, with the schools closed for five to six weeks. This was a nightmare time for some parents (especially Mam with the likes of Geordie). Back then there was no such thing as going away on holiday. Your holiday consisted of the backyard, the back lanes, the park at the top of the street and, of course, trying to keep out of trouble.

The park at the top of the street is still there some seventy years later; even today there are a few swings and very little else, no grass, only tarmac. Little wonder that the kids were always in trouble.

There were street gangs, but not like the kind we see today, who often carry knives and such. Back then, kids would make 'basters' by rolling newspapers into the shape of a tennis ball, then tying string around the ball to swing it above their heads as they charged down a rival gang's back lane.

The only time someone got hurt was because of one older kid in the back lane who was a bit of a bully. He decided to place a stone inside his baster and then struck a kid on his forehead. The kid dropped to the ground, on his back, and laid there, not moving, with an egg-shaped bump on his head growing bigger as everybody stood around in shock.

Then someone shouted, 'He's deed. Yiv killed him.'

Everybody ran like hell in all directions, leaving the poor kid flat out in the back lane. The bully kept low for a while.

One of Geordie's mob, while they were in the back lane kicking the ball around, asked, 'Di yi think he's deed?'

They all looked at Geordie who answered, 'How the hell div ah nar, but wi al nah who did it … in it wasn't me!'

A few days later they found out that he was okay, but his dad was looking for the one that had done it. No one mentioned it again, and everyone soon forgot about it.

~

Halfway through the summer holidays they were fed up with playing in the back lane and the park and, once again, they tried to get into the school playground. The grounds were still well locked, so someone suggested they to go to King Edward Street School, which was only a few hundred yards along the main road.

As they passed the store where Geordie had been caught, someone wisecracked, 'Look Geordie there's ya favourite shop.'

'Shut up you idiot,' he replied as they carried on walking along the main road.

Getting into King Edward Street School was easy, as it had a low wall that they could hop over without any problem, in to the big triangular yard. They were soon kicking the ball around; the only problem was a very heavy slope that ran down from the top of the yard toward the school building. As they were messing around, some older kids arrived and decided they would have a kickabout with Geordie's ball. One of them gave the ball a hard kick. It went flying up into the air and landed on the school roof, then rolled down into the cast-iron gutter, where it lodged itself.

They walked away, laughing, 'You can have your ball back now … if you can get it.'

Not to be beaten, Geordie walked toward the drainpipe, which was about forty-feet high. He placed one small hand on it, saying, 'I can climb that nee bother.'

'Nah, leave it Geordie. It's too high, you'll kill ya-sel,' shouted one of his little mob.

Geordie took no notice and started to climb. He had no fear of heights and was soon at the top of the drainpipe, trying to get up on to the slate roof.

He looked along the gutter and he could see a couple of other balls, but his was too far along for him to reach it. He threw the nearer balls down to his mates, and then decided he'd had enough and started to make his way back down. Then he heard shouting from below. It was the caretaker. Suddenly, he felt the strange sensations in his body. He looked down and the schoolyard looked very close, but the caretaker and his mates looked very small. He knew he was about to take a fit. By now he had learnt to sit down somewhere where he wouldn't hurt himself. Geordie stopped going down and started to blank out.

One of his mates shouted out, 'He's taking one of his fits.'

'He's going to fall,' shouted another.

As Geordie came out of the fit, he did what he normally did, he went limp for about thirty seconds. But this meant he let go of the drainpipe and came tumbling down, hitting the concrete playground with a thud. The caretaker told his mates to stay with him while he ran to phone for an ambulance.

One of his mates shouted, 'I'm ganning ti get eh's mam. Ye stay with im.' She ran like a bat out of hell along the main road and down the side street into their back lane, straight into Geordie's backyard and up the bare wooden stairs leading into Geordie's kitchen.

Geordie's Mam, seeing her so out of breath, knew something was wrong, as the kids never came into other people's houses without being told it was okay. 'What is it pet? Has he had another fit?'

Gasping for breath his mate shouted, 'Yiv got ti come quick. Yor Geordie's fell off the roof.'

Thinking she meant he'd fallen off the backyard roof, which was not that high, Mam said, 'Well you go and tell him to get himself in here now. I want to see him.'

She was nearly in tears as she shouted at Mam, 'Nah, nah. He's fell off the top of King Edward School roof. He's not moving. Yi'v got ti come now.'

Mam ran out of the kitchen – still in her slippers, pinny and turban – down the back stairs and along the main road, like a woman possessed. Geordie's mate tagged along at the back. When Mam finally got to him, she received the shock of her life. His little limbs were spread out of shape, he was unconscious, and one side of his face was so swollen that he didn't even look like Geordie. But she knew fine well not to move him. She knelt down on the concrete and stroked his head, telling him he'd be all right.

The caretaker told her an ambulance was on its way, he started to tell her that he had tried to catch him but that he'd come down too fast, but Mam wasn't listening.

It wasn't long before the ambulance came driving into the school yard, through the double gates the caretaker had opened. The ambulance men took one look at him and one of them said, 'Jesus.'

Slowly and carefully they moved him on to the stretcher. Geordie half-opened his eyes for a brief second, trying to say 'Mam', but he slipped back into unconsciousness. He vaguely heard his Mam saying, 'It's alreet son, you're going to be alreet. Don't worry.' Then her voice faded away.

For the rest of that day and most of the evening Mam waited at the hospital to hear from the doctors. One of the neighbour's kept an eye on the kids, so Dad took her shoes and coat to the hospital the minute he heard about it after he'd finished work. All the neighbours knew it must be bad as she'd been there for hours, plus they'd heard what had happened from Geordie's two mates.

Eventually, a doctor came and spoke to Mam and Dad. He told them that Geordie was on the critical list. Mam asked him what that meant, she knew it was serious, but she wanted more detail. She was not going to be fobbed off with a simple sentence, Mam was too long in the tooth for that. So, the doctor sat her down and explained that Geordie was unconscious and had not come around since being brought in; that he had broken both his arms and both his legs; that his back was badly bruised, and although it didn't look as if his spine was damaged, they could not say if, or how much, it may have affected his nervous system; that his face was swollen; that it didn't look as if he had broken any part of his skull but that in all probability he had severe concussion. At the end of that list he told Mam that he couldn't emphasise enough how serious it was, and that they needed him to come around before they could say or do anything else.

Mam couldn't stop herself asking, 'Is my lad going to die? Be honest with me doctor.'

'We desperately need your son to wake up. If he doesn't there is a possibility that he could drift into a coma. I really cannot say any more than that. Do you both understand what I am telling you?'

Mam merely nodded her head. The doctor advised them to go home and get some sleep and that hopefully there'd be good news in the morning. Mam wanted to stay, but Dad insisted that she needed to sleep and that she could come back first thing in the morning.

~

Mam lay awake late that night, waiting for the morning to come. She was up before anyone else was awake. After making their breakfast and getting them off to school, she arranged for her neighbour to keep an eye on the youngest one while she went back to the hospital. Her mind was all over the place as she walked through the hospital entrance.

The first thing she asked a nurse was, 'Was Geordie all right?'

The nurse replied that she would have to speak to the doctor and asked her to take a seat while she went to fetch him. By this time her nerves were right on the edge with all the things that had been running through her mind all night. When she had nodded off for a brief moment, she'd woken with a fright, seeing him falling through the air from a three-storey building, then hitting the concrete below with a thud. She couldn't get the image out of her head.

The doctor came into the room and Mam stood up, waiting for him to speak.

'Good news, your son woke early this morning. He has spoken to us, which is a good sign. We will have to do some tests and take some X-rays of his head and spine over the next few weeks. He will be here for some months at the very least, but things are looking a lot better than yesterday. According to his medical records, your son is epileptic, you didn't mention that.'

Mam apologised and told the doctor she'd forgotten about it in all the worry. The doctor was curious about how long he had been an epileptic and how it had come about. She gave him a breakdown of how and when it had happened. He also asked what type he was. Mam didn't quite understand what he meant as the only type she knew about was what happened when Geordie took one. Mam did tell him that after taking a fit he was back to his old self after a few minutes.

The doctor saw that Mam was still on edge and wanting to see Geordie, so he took her to the door of his room. She saw him lying in the hospital bed with his two legs in plaster casts hanging up in the air; both his arms were in plaster casts; he had a collar around his neck; the side of his face was still swollen and covered in some kind of cream. Mam took one look at him and inhaled in fright. She came up to his bed and put her hand on the top of his head.

Geordie opened his eyes and whispered, 'Sorry Mam!'

'This'll teach yi not to go doing a daft thing like climbing,' she told him and with tears in her eyes she continued to stroke his head saying, 'You'll be all right son, divint worry. I'm here, you're going to be alreet.'

Geordie closed his eyes, relieved that his Mam was there.

Over the next few weeks the X-rays and tests revealed that he had not damaged his spine or his skull. The swelling in his face started to go down, but his face and back were so badly bruised, they would take more time to clear. So, all Mam had to worry about was the healing of his arms and legs.

Mam did discover that she'd been giving Geordie his medication the wrong way. She saw a nurse simply pop the Epanutin capsule straight into his mouth without opening it. When Mam asked her about it the nurse told her that was the correct way to administer capsules. So, from that day onward that was how Mam gave Geordie his medication.

It was over three months before he was finally discharged from hospital. He walked out of there, with Mam walking beside him.

~

Not long after, Geordie found himself back in school, much to the displeasure of the teachers, as he was still taking fits, in and out of the classroom. Mam might have had a break from worrying about his fits and his getting into trouble, but it had put him way back with his education. He wasn't ever going to be top of the class at the best of times but this spell away from school didn't help him at all.

Every dinnertime he had to nip home to take his medication, as Mam couldn't trust him to take it himself. That wasn't too bad for Geordie, but it meant that his Mam was tied to being at home for him every day of the week. Like everyone else, she had other things to do to subsidise the housekeeping money – and she liked to get out of the house now and again. Small cleaning jobs helped a lot. As did a visit to the pawnshop every Monday morning with Dad's suit, which brought in ten shillings, but which had to be retrieved on the Friday. When she went to the pawnshop she always used the back entrance – Geordie went with her on many of these occasions.

~

One Sunday afternoon the following year, Geordie and his mates were playing football in the back lane with the kids from the next street. Geordie was the goalkeeper when he took a fit. The other side shot at goal with Geordie on the ground and nobody taking any notice of him, they were so used to seeing him that way. The other team jumped up and down, shouting, 'Goal, goal!'

Geordie's best mate shouted back that it didn't count cos their goalie was having a fit.

The leader of the other side answered, 'Well, if wor goalie takes a fit and you score we'll let yi count it as a goal. Okay?'

Geordie's mate pointed his finger at their goalie and shouted, 'Yi better take a fit mind, or that goal won't count.'

They went back to playing football. Geordie's mate shot at goal but the goalkeeper saved it. His mate picked the ball up shouting, 'Right, that's it, we win cos he didn't take a fit.'

The other side shouted back that they had won and walked out of the back lane.

~

His seizures (as his Mam had started to call them) were not getting any better, plus he was still getting into bother, up to a point that Dad was beginning to give up trying to keep him out of trouble, plus the fact that he wasn't afraid of his Dad's belt. To this day he doesn't know how the following occurred.

Mam sat him down in the kitchen and asked him how would he like to go to a special kind of school? He asked what she meant by special. Mam told him that it was a school that would bring his education up to everybody else's level and, on top of that, they would help to cure him of his fits.

'I'm nee further back than anybody else, ind I'm better than some others.'

But it was that last bit that Mam had said which made him sit up and listen. He was fed up taking these fits all the time, plus the fact that he didn't like the sensation he had before taking one of them.

'When will I have ti gann ti this school?' he asked.

'Oh, divant worry aboot that son. It could be a while yet.'

'Aye right, alreet Mam.' And he didn't give it another thought.

His Mam was pleased that he hadn't put up an argument for not wanting to go.

The following day at school he told his little mob all about what Mam had told him. Although he never mentioned anything about education, he just told them it was like you see on the pictures, like a holiday with the sea and the beaches. Plus, they were going to stop him taking fits cos it was a special school.

'Harra-way, yiv done someick rang again ind there sending yi away. Yee cannit kid us Geordie.'

He tried to tell them otherwise, but they wouldn't believe him. One of his mates asked if they were going to cut his head open and give him shocks with lightning, like in the film *Frankenstein*.

'How the hell do I know?' he replied.

'Well if it was my heed, I'd be asking me Mam,' cried one of them.

'Aw hell, will yi just forget aboot it,' Geordie told them as the bell went to return to class.

Before long the Easter break came around. That was when Mam told him that after the school break he would be going to the special school she'd told him about. He just stood there, thinking about everything his mates had been asking. Now he was beginning to have doubts about it.

'I'm not sure if I want to go now Mam.'

'Eh! I've already told the people that you were going Geordie.'

'Can wi not change wah minds.'

'Me and your Dad would get in a lot of trouble if we did that son. And you wouldn't want that would you?'

Geordie just shook his head, 'No Mam.'

His Mam had been hoping that he would go without any fuss, knowing how awkward he could be if he wanted.

~

As the school holiday came to an end, they were all in the back lane, when it was time to go indoors, what with school the following morning.

'Well, we'll see yi when yi come back wi ya knew heed Geordie,' shouted his best mate.

'Aye, that's if wi can recognise yi that is.'

'See yi Geordie.'

He stood on his own, looking around his back lane, not a soul in sight and as quiet as a grave. Then the voice of his Mam, shouting for him to come in, echoed around him.

The following morning, he was up well before his time to go to school. Then he remembered that today was the day he started his special school. He looked at the clothes his Mam had laid out for him the night before on the kitchen bench. He couldn't tell if they were brand new, but they looked it, with the exception of the coat. Inside the collar it looked like someone's name had been rubbed out and his name put in place, plus the fact that the sleeves were too long and covered half his hands.

Mam had said, 'That's alreet, we'll just tuck them under.'

There were no kids around when they left to catch the bus at the top of the street. They sat on the bus surrounded by men going to work, mainly to the pits or to the shipyards on the Tyne. They turned a few glances with Geordie being so spick and span, not that it bothered him or his Mam. He simply stared back at them.

They entered Newcastle Central Station and there, as arranged, they met up with a gentleman whom Geordie guessed was from the Gateshead Education Department. Even to this day he doesn't really know who this gentleman was representing.

They walked over a small bridge to catch the train on the other side of the station. They didn't have to wait long before a train pulled alongside. By this time Geordie was very apprehensive about what was happening.

At that point, Mam knelt down to face him, 'Geordie son, listen to me, you have to go with this gentleman. He's taking you to your new school.'

She didn't get a chance to finish as Geordie broke out in tears, crying that he didn't want to go and that he wanted to go back home.

'But you've got to go son, else we'll get into trouble.'

It was no good, he clung to his Mam around her waist, refusing to let go. He shouted through his tears that he would be good.

'I promise Mam, I promise I won't be bad anymore. Please don't give me away, Mam. Please Mam, don't.'

It was all too much for her and she broke down in tears at the thought of him leaving, thinking in his little mind that she didn't want him anymore.

Mr King was in the doorway of the train, ushering her to pass Geordie up to him. She picked him up and walked across to Mr King, who had to pull him away from his Mam. Once he had a hold of him, he quickly stepped backwards and slammed shut the carriage door. Geordie banged on the door with his tiny fists. People all around watched the ruckus. Mr King told him to go to the big window to see his Mam. He ran through the carriage, looking out the windows for her. She stood there, crying her eyes out as the train started to move slowly out of the station until they could no longer see each other.

Mam left the station broken-hearted at the fact that his last thought was that she no longer wanted him, that she was giving him away because he was always in trouble.

CHAPTER 4

EORDIE HADN'T SPOKEN one word as the train flashed past houses and back lanes. Then there were fewer back lanes, replaced by fields with sheep and cattle in them.

Mr King offered him sandwiches and pop. He just shook his head and looked out of the window. At any other time, this would have been like some great adventure to him, especially if his mates had been with him, but he simply felt sick to his stomach. He was missing home, missing his mates and, most of all, missing his Mam.

Mr King did his best to console him when he gave him his midday medication, but to no avail. Shortly after that he fell asleep. The next thing he knew Mr King was shaking him gently, telling him they had to get off. When the train shuddered to a halt, he handed Geordie the brown paper parcel tied with string his Mam had given him. Once off the train Mr King kept a tight hold of his small hand, in the other he held a small briefcase.

Walking through the station Geordie saw a sign telling him he was at King's Cross. People were hurrying and dashing all over the place.

'It wouldn't take much to get lost around here,' he thought to himself.

Before he knew it they were standing on stairs that were moving on their own and going down into the ground. At the bottom of the stairs he was even more surprised to see trains. He couldn't understand how they got trains under the ground. The only trains he knew were the ones at the bottom of his street. He'd never heard of the London Underground.

Before long they we going up another flight of moving steps and he found himself in another railway station, called Paddington Station.

Mr. King stood looking around, 'Ah, there we are George.'

He walked toward two large swanky buses, where a lot of other kids were waiting to get on. One thing he did notice was that boys were in the front bus and girls were for the bus at the rear.

Mr. King spoke to the one in charge. He took some papers out of his briefcase, which they both signed and he gave the nurse a copy. Geordie stood still, not knowing what was going on. To Geordie she looked like some kind of nurse in a white pinny and what looked like a nurse's hat.

Mr. King knelt in front of him, 'This good lady will be looking after you and you have to do whatever she tells you. Now you be good George and I hope we meet again.'

He stood up, shook the nurse's hand, gently tapped Geordie on the head, smiled and walked back into the station. At that point someone tried to take Geordie's parcel away from him, but he wasn't having any of that and he hung on tight – it was his Mam's parcel. The nurse looked down at him and told him to give it to the driver. The driver tugged it away and slung it on top of all the other suitcases. The nurse told Geordie to get on the bus, in no polite way.

He climbed up the stairs and stared down the aisle at them all sitting, not talking to one another, looking out the windows, smartly dressed, hair combed, and wondered what his little back lane lot would have made of them. He walked along and placed himself next to a lad who looked about his age.

It was the other lad who spoke first, 'You new?'

Geordie didn't understand what he had said and simply stared at him.

The lad spoke again, slowly, 'Are, you, a, new, boy?'

Geordie replied in his strong Geordie accent, 'What di yi mean, new?'

'Shit, where the bleedin heck you from then?' replied the cockney kid, eyes wide.

They couldn't understand a word each was saying, and sat eyeing each other up as if they were going to have a scrap.

Before the bus pulled out of the station the nurse stood at the front with a clipboard in her hands. She was a lot older than his Mam, she was old enough to be his granny. The cockney mumbled something that Geordie still didn't understand.

'Silence,' she shouted.

The cockney whispered, 'There's no bleedin one talkin.'

'I shall now take the roll,' and she called out each boy's name, who replied with either a 'yes', a 'here', or a 'present'. Eventually she called out Geordie's name. He didn't answer. Again, she called out his name, still he didn't answer. She walked down the aisle to where he was sitting. Everyone turned around as she passed. The cockney gave him a nudge as she came closer and slid down into his seat with a little moan. She looked down at Geordie and pushed her face right up to his, practically touching nose to nose.

'When I call out your name you answer me like everyone else. Do you hear me boy?'

Geordie never flinched or moved an inch, He simply stared at her, shaking his head from side to side.

'I will take it you're telling me you don't understand?'

Geordie carried on shaking his head, thinking that if his Mam had been there she would have taken her like a dog with a bone for talking to her lad like that.

She looked at the cockney, 'And I've got my eye on you, troublemaker.'

The cockney slid further down his seat.

She then called out to the driver, 'Right then, off we go driver please, seeing as we all seem to be accounted for.'

The bus was soon out of the station and travelling through the streets of London. Then London was behind them, and all he could see was fields, farms and some grand-looking houses, the likes of which he had never seen before. He had no idea where they were taking him.

The bus went through a large entrance with stone pillars holding up two very fancy, huge iron gates. On the left side of the entrance stood a towering obelisk. It seemed to Geordie to be reaching for the sky.

The nurse jumped up and shouted, 'On three you start singing. One, two, three.'

About half of the kids on the bus started to sing:

'Here we are again

Happy as can be

Jolly good friends

In jolly good company.'

That song would stay in Geordie's mind for years. Not because he liked it, simply because each time it was sung the words became more and more false.

The cockney had sunk further down into his seat, showing Geordie what he thought of it all by holding his nose. Geordie was to learn that the singing was for the benefit of the people in charge, who were in the main building.

The buses stopped outside what looked like one massive house, but turned out to be two large houses, the length of all the houses in his own street. He had never seen houses like them before, with huge windows and massive, well-tended gardens all around.

As everyone started to get off the bus a big bloke, dressed in a black suit and waistcoat, tried to keep the boys moving. The girls from the bus behind went into the house next door. Cockney stood watching the girls get off their bus. Geordie stood next to him, not knowing what to do and waiting to follow Cockney. He saw Cockney give a small wave to one of the girls. But nobody was allowed to hang around, and the big bloke grabbed Cockney by one of his ears and pulled him toward the entrance.

'Yow!' cried out Cockney, not expecting it.

The big bloke shouted, 'I see you're back. Get in there.' Then he pointed his finger first at Geordie, then toward the door entrance. 'That goes for you too – now get in.'

Geordie's mind was going like the clappers, 'If he dares touch me, I'm oot that front door and across that field heading for yem.'

He followed Cockney into a big room with three large tables and benches.

The big bloke told everyone to keep quiet, and then said, 'Everyone who knows where their beds are go to their dormitory and get changed.'

Only Geordie and three other kids were left. They stood and looked at each other, not knowing what to do. A few minutes later the same bloke came back carrying some clothes.

He just said, 'Follow me.'

Geordie walked after him in silence, followed by the other three. They went down a corridor with doors leading off it. At the bottom of the corridor he turned left into a dormitory with fifteen single beds – and a boy standing beside all but one of them.

The big bloke stopped at the third bed on the right, threw a pair of khaki shorts, a shirt and a pair of grey socks on it, turned to Geordie and told him that was his bed and he was to get changed into his clothes, same as everyone else, and that he was to wear the plimsoles that were under the bed. He then told the other three kids to follow him and they left the dormitory like sheep.

Geordie put on the khaki trousers and the shirt and the grey socks. His good pair of shoes had been replaced with what they called sandshoes where he was from. He could see that the others had folded their own clothes into neat little piles, so he did his best to do the same but made a right hash of it. He had never in his life folded his clothes into a neat little pile.

He saw Cockney had the corner bed, with no windows next to him. At least he had a window and could see outside, not that there was much to see. Just the road they'd come in on and part of the entrance to the girl's house next door.

The big bloke came back into the bedroom dormitory and told everyone, 'Outside on to the play field and get some fresh air into your lungs.'

Geordie followed the others. Once outside they walked on to the field, a matter of yards away from the building.

Cockney walked up to him full of questions, 'So then, where'd you say you came from?'

'I'm from Gateshead.'

'Never 'eard of it.'

'Where you from like?' asked Geordie.

'Me? I'm from Camden Town, London.'

'Never hord of it.'

'Fought you told me you'se were from Newcastle.'

'I am, cos they're next ti each other, cos they're both on the Tyne,' Geordie replied.

Cockney paused, 'So, you're a Geordie? What's your name then? You've got to 'ave a name.'

'Me name's Geordie.'

'Yeah, yeah. I bleedin well know that you're a Geordie, but what's your name I'm askin.'

'That is me name. Are ye thick or wat?'

'That's not what they'll call you here mate,' Cockney told him.

'What's this place called anyway?'

Cockney told him he would have to start trying to talk a bit more English for people to understand him.

'Where am I?' He asked again, looking around.

'Bleedin hell. Don't you know? Didn't anybody tell you where you were bein sent to.'

'Me Mam said it was a special school, ind that they wor ganning ti cure me of me fits.'

Cockney started to laugh, although he only understood half of what he heard. Geordie didn't like anyone taking the mickey out of him and any other time and place he would have been scrapping with him for laughing.

But Cockney could see that Geordie didn't like him laughing at him, 'Sorry Geordie. I wasn't laughin at you, it was what you said about this place goin to cure you of your fits. Leastways, I think that's what you said.'

'Why is that not reet like?'

'Look Geordie, I'll try and tell you about what this place is, and I'll do my best to keep you right before you end up gettin a good hidin.'

'Ind whose ganna give is a good hiding like?' Geordie asked, pulling his shoulders back.

'You saw that big bloke, didn't you? Let's just say don't do anythin wrong in front of him or when he's around.'

'Why? What's he ganna dee like?'

'What? I didn't understand that,' replied Cockney.

Geordie asked him again, doing his best to make himself understood. Cockney tried to explain why he didn't want to get on the wrong side of the bloke, and told him a few other things about the place and people.

'Who was the nurse on the bus?' Geordie asked.

'Ah, she's not a nurse, she's called Sister Tate, and she's in charge of the house and everyone in it, includin all the staff.'

'Staff? Wot yi mean?'

'I mean she's in charge of everyone. She has the last say about anythin. Oh, I nearly forgot, you have to address her as SISTER Tate. Did you see the name above the door when you came? It's called Tate House.'

'What! Yi mean it's hor hoose?'

'Geordie, will you try and talk bleedin English.'

At that moment, the big bloke came to the edge of the field, blowing a loud whistle.

'Come on Geordie, time for supper.'

They headed for the house, only this time they went in the back entrance.

Geordie was starving. He hadn't eaten since leaving home. He sat himself down next to the Cockney kid, on one of the benches at the long wooden table. There were plastic spoons laid out, but no oilcloth like his Mam used on her table. Someone had wheeled a large container into the dining room and had placed a plate of something in front of everyone. Geordie wasn't sure what it was, it looked like porridge. He picked up the spoon and stirred it. He was about to taste it when Cockney tugged on Geordie's elbow to stop him.

Sister Tate announced, 'We will now say grace.'

The room echoed with, 'For what we are about to receive we thank thee O Lord.'

Then everyone dived into what was in front of them with nothing said about it. Geordie took a mouthful. It smelt revolting and it tasted revolting. In his disgust, he spat it back into the plate and partly on the table. He pushed the plate away from him toward the middle of the table, spilling some more. The big bloke was quick off the mark and stepped forward to push the plate back in front of him.

'Eat it when you're told to. Now get on with it.'

He glared at Geordie.

Up until then, only Cockney had heard him speak. Sister Tate stood watching. Cockney tried to whisper 'eat it' but Geordie just stared at the big bloke, who began to lose patience. He was used to these kids doing what they were told, with no questions asked. When Geordie made no attempt to pull the plate back in front of him, he bent right over the table and did it for him, shouting, 'Eat it when you're told to.'

Geordie pushed the plate away that hard the contents went all over the table as his plate hit the plate of the boy sitting in front of him. At the same time, he stood up in defiance of being told to do something that he didn't want to by a total stranger and bellowed, 'AH DIVINT WAN IT. IT'S MUCK. IN A WANNA GAN YEM.'

No one spoke or moved as they all stared at him in total surprise. Even Cockney looked on in amazement at what was happening.

Making it quite obvious to Geordie that she had the last shout about what went on around here, Sister Tate stepped in quickly, 'Mr Hopwood, just leave it for now please.'

Geordie and Hopwood continued to stare at each other. Without looking at Sister Tate, Hopwood replied, 'Yes, Sister if that's what you wish.'

He wasn't used to being spoken back to and although he hadn't understood a word of what Geordie had shouted, he knew it wasn't anything polite.

Sister Tate quietly said something to Mr Hopwood and they left the room. Everyone started whispering to each other.

Cockney turned to his new friend, 'Bleedin hell Geordie, it's a wonder he didn't drag you out screamin. Nobody's never stood up to Mr Hopwood like that since arv been ere.'

'Heed have ti catch me forst ti dee that.'

Geordie was as proud of how fast he was, as he was of his climbing. Mr Hopwood, or anyone else for that matter, would find it hard to get hold of him.

Sister Tate and Mr Hopwood came back into the room and everyone went silent. Sister Tate used a finger to beckon Geordie over, 'You, come with me.'

He got up to follow her, keeping one eye on Mr Hopwood, whose eyes followed him all the way out of the room. Sister Tate took him into a smaller room that reminded him of Mr May's headmaster's office.

She sat him down and started talking.

'Did he know where he was and why he was there?'

He told her that his Mam had told him it was a special school, and that he would be able to catch up with his lost schooling and they were going to cure him of his fits.

'Well George, we are here to help you to try and catch up with your schoolwork. And we will do our best to eventually reduce some of your seizures. But it does take time. It doesn't happen overnight.'

'How lang div a have ti stay here?'

'I'm sorry George, I didn't quite understand what you said. Perhaps if you spoke a bit more slowly it might help us.'

There was a knock at the door and she called out for them to come in. The door opened on Mr Hopwood. Geordie was up on his feet like a shot, his eyes flashing to see if he could get past him out of the door. Sister Tate could see how uptight he was.

'It's alright George. No need to worry. Mr Hopwood has brought you some sandwiches and a glass of milk.'

'Is there anything else Sister?' Hopwood asked, not giving Geordie a second glance.

'Not here Mr Hopwood, but if you could start getting the boys ready for bed it would be a great help while I finish talking to George.'

'Certainly Sister,' and he closed the door behind him.

'Now, where were we George? Ah yes, I was trying to say that we are going to have a bit of difficulty understanding what you are saying owing to your strong accent and dialect. So, rather than all of us trying to talk as you do, which would be rather difficult, maybe it would be better if you tried to talk the King's English, so that we can understand each other.'

He knew what she was telling him but said nothing.

So Sister Tate went on, 'Is this the first time you've been away from home George?'

He shook his head to indicate that it was not. Her curiosity was aroused so she asked, 'Was it another place like this one?'

'I was in hospital,' he replied.

'And why were you in hospital George. Was it to treat you for your fits?'

'No, I fell off the school roof.'

'Oh, I see. And were you very hurt when you fell.'

'I was in hospital for a long long time. I had my legs and arms in plaster.'

She tutted. 'Was that the only time you were away from home?'

He shook his head once more.

'Ah, and why where you away from home that time?'

He told her that the police had sent him to a remand home for being bad.

'What did you do for them to do that George?'

'I think it was because I was keep getting into trouble with them.'

Then she asked what it was like where he lived. Geordie wasn't sure what she wanted to know, so he told her, 'I live with me Mam and Dad, and me brothers and sisters, upstairs in the bedroom and kitchen. The hooses are all the same. We play in the back lanes ind the streets.'

'And can I ask what your dad does.'

'I divent know what yi mean.'

'I mean what does your dad do for his work?'

'Aw, he works doon the pit.'

'You mean he's a miner.'

'Nah, he works doon the pit digging oot coal.'

'I think that's enough for the night. We'll have another chat later on. But I can tell you George, if you behave yourself while you're here at Chalfont Colony, you'll be all right. You'll just need to settle in, that's all.'

'Can I ask how lang have I got to stay here for?'

Sister Tate paused, 'Well now, that would depend on how we get along while you are here, and somehow I'm sure we'll get along fine. If you follow me, I'll show you what to do.'

He followed her back to his dormitory, where she told him to change into his pyjamas, then to follow the rest of the boys who were brushing their teeth, then to go back to his bed.

This was the first time he'd ever brushed his teeth. He'd never seen a toothbrush or toothpaste before. Geordie looked in the mirror at his teeth, they were half-rotten, especially the back ones.

Sister Tate came around, giving each boy his medication. She smiled at Geordie as she popped his into his mouth. Then she stood at the entrance of the dormitory and called out, 'Prayers everyone.'

They all jumped out of their beds and knelt at the side. Geordie copied and listened to what he later knew was the

Lord's Prayer. He was beginning to learn that a prayer was said before every meal, every night, and in church every Sunday. After prayers they all climbed back into their beds.

As Sister Tate left the dormitory, she called out, 'And no talking!'

It was still light outside; Geordie couldn't understand why they were going to bed so early. He lay in bed thinking about home and his mates and how much he was missing it. His heart felt heavy as a lump of lead and he wondered how long he could stand this way of life. He silently started to cry. That first night he had two fits, probably brought on by the stress of wanting to be home and being in such a strange place.

CHAPTER 5

THE FOLLOWING MORNING they were all up at seven o'clock. He got dressed once again in the khaki shirt and short trousers, grey socks and plimsoles.

He followed Cockney, who told him they were to brush their teeth again. Geordie asked why, as they'd done it before going to bed last night. Cockney told him they had to do it every morning and night. Geordie couldn't understand why they had to do it every day, never mind twice a day.

Breakfast began with prayers, followed by scrambled egg and brown bread – which Geordie couldn't get used to. As they ate, Cockney told him that he'd heard Geordie taking his fits during the night.

'Never seen anyone take fits like that before.'

'How'd you mean?' Geordie asked. 'I thought everybody was the same.'

'No way. You started by groanin your head off and then curled up like a ball.'

'What aboot that bloke who was sitting in that little office, did he come oot ind have a luck?'

'Listen mate, think yourself lucky he didn't. But if that skinny bastard comes anywhere near you in the middle of the night you scream your fuckin head off. You hear me Geordie?'

'Aye a hear yi. But why would a wonna dee that for?'

'Cors he's fuckin scum that's why.'

Geordie thought maybe the bloke had clipped him at some time or other, or worse, given him a good hiding. Not that it would bother him, he'd had plenty of those in the past.

'How lang yi been in this place Cockney?'

'Two year. And that's two year too fuckin long.'

After breakfast they lined up in twos outside the house, ready for school.

'Is this school very far?' He whispered to Cockney.

'It's that fuckin thing over there.' Cockney pointed to a single-storey building not more than twenty yards across the small roadway in front of the house. It didn't look much like a school to Geordie, compared to Sunderland Road Comprehensive, which housed more than 1,500 kids.

'Cockney, can you do something for me?'

'Sure, what is it mate?'

'Can you stop your fucking swearing. Every two words you say is fucking.'

'Didn't know it'd upset you that much. Don't they swear up norf?'

'Oh aye, but not as much as yee dee. The only people we hear swearing is when they're drunk.'

'Can't say I'll stop, but I'll try not to in front of you, okay?'

'Yeah, okay,' Geordie tutted.

'You know, when I think about it, me whole fuckin family swears,' muttered Cockney.

Mr Hopwood escorted them across the road and saw them into the school assembly room, where they were joined by the girls from the house next door. The headmaster, Mr Thomas, spoke to all the children and then asked the new ones to stay in assembly. He sat behind a desk and called up each child to ask where they were from, what had been the name of their school, did they know any of their times tables, could they write, and generally what lessons had they been doing at school. Although Geordie had missed out on quite a bit of schooling through being in hospital, as he stood listening to what the other kids had to say about themselves, he knew he was a lot brighter by the way they tried to answer the questions.

When the headmaster finished, he placed them into suitable classes. Geordie was pleased to see Cockney smiling at him from behind one of the desks in the room he walked into. Geordie didn't think it looked like a classroom. He did notice that all sixteen in the class were boys. When he got the chance, he asked Cockney why that was. He told him they had tried mixed classes but had changed back to separate classes for boys and girls.

'That was a pity. My girlfriend was in the same class as me, and it was the only chance we had for a bit a snoggin.'

'Why'd they change them back like?'

'Don't know really. Think some of the teachers didn't like it, somethin like that anyway.'

'My old class had aboot fifty kids in it, boys and girls,' Geordie told him.

The stocky teacher was trying to teach them maths, obviously not his best subject, when suddenly one of the boys dropped off his seat and took a fit, right in front of him. He had never seen anyone else taking a fit and it frightened Geordie to watch him on the floor. His arms were between his legs, his head was held right back as if he were trying to look behind him, his eyes were fluttering up and down, slaver was coming from his mouth and he was jerking all over the place. Geordie expected the teacher to come hurrying to help him in some way or another, but he casually walked toward him, looked down, bent over, moved him slightly away from the desk legs and then carried on with the lesson as if nothing had happened. Geordie was shocked.

The young lad was still lying on the floor when the lesson finished. It looked to Geordie as if he was sleeping.

At dinner time they marched in twos, back across to Tate House. Once again Sister Tate made them place their hands together, followed by, 'For what we are about to receive may the Lord make us truly thankful.'

The dinner consisted mainly of vegetables, which he hated, but he was so hungry he had little choice but to eat it. After dinner they were allowed to go outside and play on the field, known as Tate field. Geordie stood with Cockney, looking around. The only thing to see was a single tree.

'What di they mean go and play on the field?' asked Geordie.

'Probably play with each other I suppose,' replied Cockney.

'But there's nowt here ti play with. What wi supposed ti dee, throw grass at each other? There's nee swings or roondaboots, there's nowt. A mean, at least it the top of wor street we had a scabby bit park. There was hardly owt in it but it was betta than this load of crap.'

'Get used to it Geordie, cos this is the best you can hope for mate.'

Geordie felt depressed at the thought of it all as he turned and looked at Cockney.

'What?' Cockney asked.

'Fucking hell! I'm not staying in this shithole. I'm ganning yem the forst chance a git.'

Cockney didn't fully understand what he'd said but he had a vague idea what he'd meant. 'Geordie mate, if you're thinkin of doin a runner forget it. Nobody escapes from here, believe me when I fuckin tell you. I've tried it and I live in Camden Town, which is only in London, not a kick and a fuckin arse from here, you don't stand a cat in hell's chance of ever gettin back to – what do you call it again? Yemm.'

Geordie was looking at some kids who'd walked around the field, 'What's on the other side of that field across there?'

'Come on, I'll show you,' replied Cockney.

They walked across the field and Geordie peered through the thick bushes that had been left to grow, obviously to stop people seeing in toward the houses and school.

'Hey, that's a road through there,' cried Geordie as he pushed into the thicket to get a better look.

'Yeah, I know that. I told you, I've been here two year and there's not much I don't know about this fuckin place mate.'

'Aye well, I'll give it a while then I'm ganning back where I come from.'

'Geordie mate, you'll be picked up by the law the minute you're out on that road, I'm not kiddin. Then on top of that you've got to get to London. You saw how long it took on the bus to get here, and you'll have to walk that distance without bein spotted by the law.'

'Aye well, I'm ganna try it anyway,' Geordie replied, not wanting to show he was beaten so easily.

'Even if you get to fuckin London you've still got to get to fuckin King's Cross Station, then travel nearly 300 mile or even more? Nah Geordie mate, forget it and try and make the most of what you've got.'

'Listen Cockney, where I come from there's pits, shipyards, scrapyards, dorty back lanes, cobbled streets, railway lines it the bottom of wor street, ind muck al ower the place, but I'd rather be there than this place, cos that's yemm.'

Cockney shook his head; he knew nothing he said was going to make his new mate change his mind about trying to get back home.

~

Saturday was the highlight of the week, when pocket money was handed out to each boy after they lined up outside Tate House and then marched in twos, out of the main entrance and down a narrow lane toward some houses. Geordie received two shillings (in today's money that would be twenty pence, but it was worth a lot more then).

'Where we ganning?' he asked his mate.

'How much did she give you?' asked Cockney.

'Two bob,' replied Geordie.

Cockney looked at Geordie suspiciously, 'Fuckin hell! It took her nearly two years to give me that much. She must think you're somefinck fuckin special to be givin you top pocket money straight away.'

'Divant look at me like that. I divant nah, div ah.'

'Your old man's not rich by any chance is he?'

'Divant be daft. Me Dad works doon the pit digging oot coal. Anyways, wit does yors dee?'

'Aw me old man's never worked as long as I've known.'

'Ah! So I'm rich compared ti yee then?' Geordie laughed.

'Yeah, I suppose so,' and Cockney laughed back as they walked out the main entrance of the Colony.

'Haway then, tell us where we ganning,' Geordie asked again.

'We're gannin, as you say, to a corner shop that sells sweets.'

'Is that what these two bobs for, ti buy bullits?'

'Bullets? It's a corner fuckin shop not a gun shop,' Cockney replied.

'I didn't say bullets I said bullits.'

Cockney shook his head, 'Geordie mate, I think it's goin to be a while before we can really understand what you're talkin about.'

Down the narrow road, they passed a large house sitting in its own grounds. Geordie nodded toward it, 'I'd like a hoose like that one day.'

'In your dreams Geordie, in your dreams.'

'Ah divint nah aboot that.'

In the near distance Geordie could see what looked like council houses he'd seen in Gateshead with tiny front gardens. In front of them were two corner shops facing each other. One was a small sweet shop, the other was a greengrocer, with flowers, small plants and fruit on display outside. Separating the two shops was a dirt road that led up toward the houses.

The kids knew the drill and lined up outside the sweet shop. Sister Tate went inside and the kids followed, two at a time. The kids outside started to jostle each other, eager to be the next two in the shop.

Geordie watched what was happening inside the tiny corner shop. He could see the ones being served by the lady behind the counter pointing to the jar of sweets they wanted, and handing over their pocket money. As one of the kids came out of the shop, he took a look to see what he'd got for his money, and Geordie asked him, 'How much?' The kid replied, 'One and six,' clutching his tiny bag tight to his chest.

'It's alreet, I'm not ganna pinch them!'

Geordie's little mind kicked in as he watched each kid turning over his pocket money for a tiny bag of sweets. 'Who's getting what from who?' As Sister Tate called out for the next two kids. Cockney and Geordie pushed themselves to the front, much to the displeasure of the rest. He pointed to what he wanted saying, 'A quarter of them.' The lady handed him a small packet of sweets, he looked at her again, 'And a quarter of those.'

The lady gave Sister Tate a glance, who quickly intervened, 'That's it, pay the lady and go outside.'

'Is that it, is that all yi git?'

Nobody had ever stood in defiance of Sister in the time that Cockney had been at the Colony. He stood there watching in awe.

'He's new,' Sister told the lady. 'Outside now!' she said to Geordie in a stern voice.

Outside he told Cockney what he thought, who said, 'It's a waste of time moanin about it. Who's goin to take any notice of you?'

Nevertheless, he felt like he'd been robbed, for once in his life the shoe was on the other foot and he didn't like it one bit. While they were waiting outside the shop three kids came down the dirt road from the houses. First, they stood looking at the kids from the Colony, then they got a bit more daring and started doing an impression as if they were all retarded.

'Who the fuck do they think they are?' cried Geordie.

Cockney told him to calm down, that they were kids from up the road who often came to take the mick, but the minute Sister came out they did a bunk.

One of them started walking around as if he were a zombie. That was enough for Geordie.

'You lot come near me and I'll rip your head off,' he walked toward them looking for a scrap. Cockney had no choice but to follow his mate, more to stop him from doing something daft than anything else. When the locals saw Geordie and Cockney coming toward them, they turned tail and ran.

'Tell yi what, if them come again ti try ind take the mick oot of me I'll be up that back lane after them. I'll git one of them bastards.'

Cockney was just pleased they were gone, as he believed Geordie when he said next time he'd be up the lane and get one of them. That would really cause some bother. He was beginning to think that his new mate was going to be a handful for Sister Tate. Most of the kids gathered in a circle around Geordie and Cockney.

On seeing the group around Geordie as she came out of the shop, Sister Tate clapped her hands twice and called out,

'Come along, come along. What's going on here? Get back into twos. Now!'

The kids shuffled into pairs, ready to start walking, when the three kids appeared up the road. Cockney saw them first, then Geordie got his eyes on them as one of them started taking the mickey out of them again. Sister Tate had seen them, but there was little she could do about it. She told the boys to carry on walking and to keep their eyes to the front.

Cockney took hold of Geordie's khaki shirt and whispered, 'Forget it Geordie. It's not worth it.'

The three kids knew that when the nurse was there, they were as safe as houses, and were now standing outside the greengrocer's shop, less than ten yards from the file of boys. Two were laughing their heads off, while the other one acted like a zombie again. Sister Tate was trying her best to hurry them along out of the situation. Trouble was, they were doing their antics at Geordie.

'Fuck them, I've had enough of this,' he shouted, as he dashed across the road toward them, his fists tight closed.

They bolted up the lane once more, only this time Geordie managed to grab the one who was taking the mickey. The two were rolling all over the dirt road as Sister Tate ran over, followed by Cockney. It took the two of them to separate the fighters. Although she didn't show it, Sister was glad that Cockney was there to give her a hand. Sister had hold of the local boy's arm and told him in no uncertain manner that she would be reporting this matter and that he would be in a lot of trouble. Then told him to get himself off home.

Geordie and Cockney stood glaring at him with looks that could kill.

'And you two, back in line. Now!'

As they marched off, Geordie and Cockney looked behind them. The three kids were standing staring, but looking a bit sorry for themselves. Geordie stuck his two fingers up at them, and all three returned his gesture. But Sister Tate was walking at the rear and saw everything.

After ten or so minutes of walking in silence Cockney, in a low voice, said, 'I think you're in deep shit Geordie. You might not have to do a runner after all. It wouldn't surprise me if they put you out the fuckin door. Fightin with a local kid. Phew!'

'Quicker the better far as I'm concerned,' he replied.

Sister Tate never once took her eyes from him all the way back to Chalfont Colony. At Tate House she told Geordie she would speak to him after tea. She was seen talking to Mr Hopwood the moment they entered Tate House. They thought it was odds on that she was telling him about the incident. Cockney told him she would be reporting to the matron about it, but he was only guessing. Geordie said that, either way he couldn't give a toss and he hoped they would send him yemm.

It was obvious that she had told Mr Hopwood about what had happened as his eyes never left Geordie all the time Sister Tate was out of sight. Even when told to go out on the field to play after their lunch, Mr Hopwood followed them. He wasn't taking any chances of Geordie absconding while he had been told to keep a sharp eye on him. A little later, Mr Hopwood shouted for him to come in from the field.

'This is it,' said Cockney. 'Good luck. You're goin to fuckin need it mate.'

Mr Hopwood just shook his head and said, 'Follow me.'

In the entrance hall he turned and knocked twice on Sister Tate's office door.

'Come in,' she called. He ushered Geordie into her office, where she was sitting behind a desk. She thanked Mr

Hopwood as he left the office. Geordie stood waiting for her to speak. Eventually, she lifted her head.

'That was disgraceful behaviour from you this morning. In all my years at Chalfont I have never witnessed such behaviour from anyone. The incident has been reported to Matron. At the moment we do not know the names of the other boys and until someone makes a complaint to us there is not much we can do about it. Meanwhile, I have to ask you to throw some light on the matter and explain to me how, and why, it happened in the first place. Why did you not ignore those three boys instead of running across to fight them?'

Geordie stood looking at her, not answering.

'WELL ANSWER ME,' she shouted.

'THEY WERE TAKING THE MICKEY,' he shouted back.

She was taken aback by his shouting at her. She had never had a boy like the one in front of her. He was a wild one.

'Calm down and sit down,' she told him.

He dragged a chair across the floor toward her desk and sat down on it. She realised that she was approaching the subject the wrong way. Matron had instructed her to find out why he had done such a thing. He'd only been at Chalfont Colony for less than a week and he was already causing chaos. She decided to approach the questioning in a different manner, and sat back in her chair.

'Well George, what are we going to do? I know they were taunting you, but could you not have ignored them?'

'I did ignore them the first time,' he told her.

She leant forward, this was something she didn't know about. 'Are you telling me that they had taunted you before you fought with one of them.'

'Aye, but they ran away when I went for them.'

'And can I ask you George, when this first part happened?'

'I divent nah. What yi mean by forst part?'

Sister was having difficulty following his Geordie dialect. Slowly she began to understand what he was telling her, which threw a different light on the whole situation. After a fairly long conversation she rounded it up by saying, 'So George, what you have told me is that while I was busy inside the sweet shop, these three boys were taking the mickey out of the children outside, and of you in particular. They ran away when you went to approach them, then when we were ready to leave they taunted you again. Incidentally, I did see their antics and what they were doing in trying to belittle you and the other boys. I take it that was all you could take from them?'

Geordie nodded.

'Right then, we'll leave the matter there and I'll inform Matron of everything that happened.'

When Sister stood up, so did Geordie.

'Can I ask yi a question? Will a be ganning yem now?'

'George, could you say that again in a way that I can understand? And say it slowly.'

Geordie gave a heavy sigh and repeated himself, 'Will I be ganning – erm – back – home – now?'

'Oh, I see what you're asking. Will you be going back home now? This morning I would have said "yes", but after talking to you I really don't know. We'll tell you one way or the other in the next few days.'

As she opened the door for him, she said, 'Right, back on to the field and keep out of trouble. Do you hear me?'

He didn't answer her, but for that brief moment she reminded him of his Mam – di yi hear me?

Back on the field Cockney watched him come out of Tate House and ran across, 'Well? What she say? Are you gettin the boot or what?'

'Yor guess is as good as mine. How the hell div ah nah.'

'Aw, here we bleedin go again. Listen Geordie, tell me what she asked you.'

'I told hor a ran ti put one on him cos they wor taking the mickey.'

'And did you tell her it was the second time they had stood there takin the mick out of you.'

'Aye, ah did. She was more interested aboot what happened when she was inside the shop than owt else.'

'There we are then,' replied Cockney.

'What di yi mean? What yi trying ti say like.'

'She's just tryin to cover her own backside, ain't she?'

'Is she? Ah divint see how yi make that oot.'

'Listen, the fact they took the mickey not once but twice gets her off the hook.'

'Ah divint nah what the hell yor trying ti tell us.'

'Crickey, listen will you. If they've taken the mickey once they might say she didn't have control of what was goin on, but because they came back and did it again, then it became their fault not yours – or hers. Do you see what I mean?'

'Ah, a git what yi mean,' said Geordie. 'You're telling me I've blown me chances of – how yee put it? – gitting the boot.'

'Yeah you could put it that way I s'pose.' Cockney was thinking more about Sister Tate than about Geordie.

The matter was never mentioned again. Cockney seemed to think that the three kids involved were more afraid of what might happen to them if they were found out. After a few weeks things settled down to the normal boring regimental routine of the Colony.

~

His new mate kept trying to speak to Shirley, his girlfriend. The only chance he ever seemed to get was at school, and only when they were changing classrooms. Contact of any kind was strictly forbidden between the sexes and, as far as the boys were concerned, sex education was out the window while Geordie was at Chalfont Colony. This did not put Cockney off from seeing Shirley every chance he could get. Geordie would keep toot (watch) for his mate while they had a few minutes snogging.

One day, Cockney told him that Shirley had a mate if he wanted a girlfriend. Geordie knew who they were referring to – she was twice as broad as him.

'Nee thanks, am not inti lasses,' he told Cockney.

'You're not a puff, are you?'

'Fuck off!'

'I was only kiddin you; can you not take a joke?'

'Well I aint a puff, so git that into ya heed.'

'I was only jokin mate.'

~

Geordie had never seen a grown-up taking a fit. The first time was on a Sunday morning, not long after he'd arrived. Every Sunday morning most people at Chalfont Colony attended church – a mixed construction of brick and mostly timber, painted black on the outside. During the service a woman fell on the floor taking a major fit. Unlike at school, the woman was carried out. It really frightened him. Was that going to be him when he was older? Boys and girls attended church, they had no option. He was never sure what religion was being taught, not that he took a blind bit of notice while he was there. Much later, Sister Tate, being Irish, asked would he like to attend Holy Communion. He hadn't got a clue what she was talking about. She told him, with vigour, that it was something she would have to look into at a later date.

He soon learnt there was a different building for washing and laundry, another for cooking all meals for the entire Colony, while others were living accommodation for the adult patients, with the sexes still strictly kept separate. They grew most of their own food on large, well-kept plots of land behind Tate House. And there was a large orchard with rows and rows of apples – on bushes rather than trees – which he later found out were Cox's apples. Geordie couldn't resist the temptation and was soon in the orchard instead of playing on the field. The apples were sweet and he gave half to Cockney.

Cockney was right about Sister Tate wanting to know more about him and his background. She took him into her study (as she called it) one Sunday after tea. Cockney told him to lay it on thick, whatever she asked about. She wanted to know if he had any brothers or sisters.

'I've got three brothers and three sisters.' Which wasn't true, at that time he only had two brothers and one sister – the rest of the family came along later.

'And do you live in a nice big house, George?'

'We live upstairs. We have a kitchen and a bedroom like everybody else.'

'So, where do you all sleep then?'

'In the bedroom. Me Mam has three beds.' Which was correct.

She was taken aback on hearing they all slept in one room, which again was very true.

'And can I ask what your father does for a living?'

'Me Dad works doon the pits digging coal.'

'Oh, you mean he's a miner.'

'Nah. He's a pitman. He digs oot coal. He works for the Coal Board. Me Dad works with me three uncles. They said if anyone hurts me that they'd all come and sort them oot.'

'Now don't you go worrying your little head about things like that. No one is going to hurt you while I'm in charge. Just one last question George. Does anyone else in your family take fits?'

'Nah, just me. I got hit on the back of me heed by a drunk throwing a beer bottle.'

'And I understand that you had an accident a while ago, is that right?'

'Yus. I fell off the school roof. I was only getting our ball back.'

'Was it very high?'

'Two times higher than this hoose. I took a fit and fell on the concrete school yard.'

'And that's why they sent you to hospital?'

'Yus, for nearly a year. I hurt me arms, me legs, me head and me back as weel.'

'Listen to me George. You and I are going to get on a great deal. You have a lot to learn, just don't get led astray by anyone and we'll get along fine. All right?'

'Yus Sister.'

'And it's not yus Sister; it's yes, Sister. Now off you go and join the others for supper.'

He had done what Cockney had told him and laid it on a bit thick with some of his answers. It didn't go wrong, to Geordie's way of thinking, to keep yourself covered.

~

It was the same one day after the other, nothing changed, the same routine. Plus the fact there was not one single piece of rubbish of any kind lying around anywhere.

On Sunday nights before bedtime Sister Tate would have all the children in the dining room, writing letters home to their parents. Geordie was desperate to get back home. Every night he would close his eyes thinking of home. One Sunday he wrote to his Mam that if you did anything wrong that they didn't like, you would end up getting a good hiding or punished in some other way. What his mate hadn't told him was that Sister Tate read every letter before it was sealed. After reading his letter she tore it up in front of him and told him if he wrote anything like that again he *would* be punished. Geordie therefore decided he would have to tell his Mam himself. Lying in bed that night he told Cockney he was heading for home tomorrow.

'Don't be fuckin daft. You haven't got a cat in hell's chance of gettin all the way back to Newcastle.'

'Well am ganna try anyways,' said Geordie, rolling over and dreaming of home.

The following night after tea the two of them were walking around the field and, once they were on the far side and true to his word, Geordie leapt into the thick privet hedge and kept going until he came out on the country lane. He looked around to see which direction to go, but couldn't see any signposts, so rather than going right, which would take him to the entrance of the Colony, he turned left. There were no cars or anything else in sight. He took the first turning on his right, which brought him out to the corner where the sweet shop was facing the greengrocer. All he needed was to bump into those three kids again, so he hurried along until he was out of sight of the shops. Turning again at the bottom of the road he was surprised to see quite a few shops and, in the middle of the road, a fair-sized pond in front of a pub. He didn't know it, but he was in the village of Chalfont St Peter. On the opposite side of the road stood a churchyard.

Back at Tate House, Sister Tate lost her cool when she found out that Geordie had gone missing from the field. She headed straight for Cockney when she first heard about it. Cockney denied any knowledge. All he told her was that Geordie was missing his Mam and friends in Newcastle.

Geordie stood staring into the shop windows, none of which were open. He stood out like a sore thumb, dressed as he was in khaki shirt and short khaki trousers and plimsoles. Who in their right mind would wear what he had on if they had a choice?

He looked around. There were only a handful of people about. He'd been walking for a couple of hours and it was now turning dark. He would have left the village, only he didn't know which way would take him to London.

'Where you off to son?'

Geordie turned around and nearly died. Sanding in front of him was a policeman. Some twenty yards away his partner was sitting in a police car. He did his best to try and hide his dialect and Geordie accent.

'Am just on me way home,' he replied.

'And where would home be then, son?'

He didn't answer simply because he didn't know what to answer. He couldn't say Gateshead and then expect them to say, 'Oh well, on your way then.'

The police car pulled alongside, 'Tell you what, jump in the back seat and we'll give you a lift.'

He knew the game was up and climbed into the back of the police car. Cockney was right, he had no way of getting back home when he was stuck in the middle of a place that was all strange to him.

It wasn't long before they pulled up outside Tate House. Sister Tate came straight outside to meet them and explained that he hadn't been with them very long and was homesick. She thanked the officers politely and sent Geordie straight to bed. He was not allowed out of it the following day, except to use the toilet. He took all his meals on his own. On Monday morning things went back to the old routine.

Cockney told him, 'She'll have someick up er sleeve for you Geordie boy. You don't get off that easy, not from her.'

After tea everyone was told to go outside to the field.

'Not you,' Sister pointed a long bony finger at Geordie. 'Off to bed until you learn the rules of this house.'

He was escorted to the dormitory by one of the duty officers, and went there every night after tea for a full week. Sitting in bed all that time made him realise that his mate was right in telling him there was no way he could get back home from where he was, stuck in Chalfont Colony. But he hadn't given up hope, not yet at least.

~

His time in Chalfont Colony passed very slowly, leastways compared to what he had been accustomed to, it was as boring as it could get. It was 'yes sir, no sir, three bags full sir'. He was still taking fits, usually at least twice a week. He hadn't seen Cockney taking one single fit during the first few months he was there. When he asked him about it he told him that for some unknown reason he took them when he was asleep. Once, when he was at home before being sent here, he nearly choked in the middle of the night while having one. He'd been at the Colony two years. He had only been at Tate House for one year and was nine months older than Geordie.

'Me Mam told me that I was being sent here to catch up with me schoolwork and to be cured.'

Cockney was older than his age as far as knowing what two and two made. 'Ha! You might catch up to your schoolwork mate but I don't know about curin you. That's a new one to me.'

'What's the point in being here if they cannit cure yi? A mean, a could have catched up ti me schoolwork back it me owled school?'

'Beats me Geordie. Why don't you ask Sister Tate? She's in charge, not me.'

'Aye well, a will if a get a chance.'

Sure enough, he got his chance the following Sunday after writing home to his Mam. He knew that Sister Tate would be reading his letter before sealing it closed. He had written his Mam that they didn't cure them at this place like they were told, and that the school was not in the same league as his old school. He knew that Sister wouldn't allow him to send it, although he had not said anything detrimental against the place. After handing his letter over he went back to the table and sat down.

Sister read the letter, looked across to him, lifted her hand and raised one finger at him to come over to her, 'When everyone goes to get ready for bed I want you to sit where you are. You and I need to have a chat.'

She then ushered him to go back and sit down.

'What the hell have you done now?' whispered his mate.

'Told me Mam they didn't cure you, it's all made up; and the school stinks.'

Cockney shook his head in disbelief.

When everyone had gone and he and Sister Tate were left alone, she got up and sat at the table facing him.

'George, have you any idea why I asked you to stay back?'

Not wanting to be punished for what he had written in his letter he replied, 'Nah Sister. I've got nee idea.'

She looked at him, trying to figure out if he was telling her the truth or not. He was one of very few boys that came to Tate House she found difficult to understand, not only in dialect, but also in nature. She had never had a boy with his background, which in itself made him a challenge.

'I asked you to stay behind because of what you have written in your letter to your mother.'

Geordie played along with what she was saying.

'I divant nah what yi mean Sister.'

'You have said in your letter that the school here is not as good as your old school. Is that right?'

'Yus Sister.'

'Can I ask how many children were in your class at your old school?'

'I think there were nearly fifty, Sister.'

'And how many are there in your class at Chalfont school?'

'I think there's about fourteen or fifteen Sister. I didn't really count them.'

'Surely that tells you George that the fewer children there are in a class must give you a far better education.'

'Yus Sister, but the teachers here aren't as good as my old school ones.'

This really made Sister Tate sit up.

'Can you explain what you mean by your old teachers being better than the Chalfont teachers.'

'I'm not sure Sister, but my old teachers always made sure you knew what the lesson was about by the time the classes changed, and if you didn't, another teacher had you for another while, or you would be kept in class at dinner time or after school to learn it.'

'Was there anything else that was different between the schools?'

'The classes wor mixed lads and lasses. And yi got the cane if yi did owt rang.'

'I understood the first part of what you said, the rest seemed all jumbled-up words. Anyway that's enough about schools. I need to talk to you about what you've written to your mother about being cured here at Chalfont.'

'Me Mam said I was being sent here to be cured. But they don't cure you, do they? And if they don't, what am I here for?'

She told him he was a clever young man, but she went on to explain that it didn't work the way he thought. That sometimes it happens over a long period of time, and for some people it didn't happen.

'So how will I know if it's working for me then?'

'You have to give it time George. But don't you worry about things like that, the quicker you start to really settle in the quicker you will find that you don't have your fits as often as you used to. Do you understand what I'm trying to tell you George?'

He thought that she was telling him a load of crap, but he didn't say so. All he replied was, 'I think so Sister.'

'Good. Now I want you to write another letter to your mother, telling her you've made some friends and that you're going to school. Can you do that for me George?'

He knew that he had no choice but to do as he was told, 'Yus Sister.'

'And George, what have I told you about your English? It's not YUS Sister, it's YES Sister.'

Once in bed, when all was quiet, Cockney was straining at the leash wanting to know why she had kept him back to have a one to one talk. Geordie told him all about it.

'Boy you've really got under her skin.'

'Aye, but why me?'

'Probably because she's never had one like you, that's why.'

'Silence in there,' called out the night duty officer, sitting in his office in between the two large dormitories. Geordie rolled over to go to sleep. It was still daylight outside as he closed his eyes, thinking of his pals, probably still playing out in the back lane or the Hykey Park or even on the railway lines. And here he was, curtains closed and being told to get to sleep. His pals would have taken all this as one big joke if he was to tell them.

The following morning, after Geordie woke, he really felt it was time for him to be looking for a way out once again.

~

But, as time went by, he began to give up all hope of getting back home. The first year at Chalfont Colony was hard for him in many ways. What with most people not understanding what he was saying, the uniformity, the way everything was done – it was all so institutionalised. But most of all it was the sheer boredom, and the humdrum way of life that got to him in the early years. Repeating the same thing, day in, day out, with no change whatsoever in the routine. Until one day Cockney asked him, was he going home for the summer holidays? At first he thought he was taking the mickey.

'You know for a fact I've already tried it,' he replied.

Cockney started to laugh. 'No, I mean are you goin home for the summer? Some of us do, but some of the kids here never get that chance.'

This was news to Geordie.

'Yeah, if your parents want you home, like for Christmas and especially the summer holidays, they let you go.'

That Sunday night George wrote to his Mam to tell her all about being allowed to come home, and that he would like to come home for summer as he was missing everyone.

As the weeks went by Sister Tate read out the names of the boys whose parents had requested their children home for the holidays. Each Sunday he sat on the edge of his stool waiting for his name to be called out. Cockney's name had been called out the week before, so the two of them waited anxiously to hear Geordie's name. And then it happened. His name was called out. He was going home at last. He didn't know when exactly, but he was going home. Sister Tate didn't show it, but Cockney made the comment that she looked pleased when she'd called out his name.

'Why would she be pleased?' Geordie asked.

'Hmm, I don't really know, but I know one thing.'

'Oh, what's that then?'

'She looked at you when she called out your name and smiled.'

'So, what's wrang wi that then?'

'That's what's puzzlin me,. Why would she smile knowin she'd given you a piece of good news?'

'Aw, a give up wi yee,' Geordie replied. He did not give a monkey's, he was going home.

That night, when everyone was saying prayers, he whispered a thank you to God.

Cockney and Geordie were as high as a kite the next day in school. Cockney couldn't wait to tell Shirley, who he gave a quick kiss to in front of a few of the school kids.

The following Sunday after letter writing Sister Tate told them that these were the names of the last few boys who were going home for the summer holiday. After she had called out four names and told everyone to carry on what they were doing, one of the boys started shouting, 'What about me? Why am I not going home? I want to go home as well!'

He was getting hysterical as everyone stood around, watching him. Sister Tate tried to calm him down, to no avail. The male attendant on duty came hurrying into the dining room. Sister gestured to him to remove the boy as he was truly out of control. The male attendant grabbed the boy by his hair and screams could be heard as he was dragged down the corridor toward the bedrooms. Everyone just stood in silence, it was something they'd remember for a long time.

~

Eventually, it was the night before the summer holidays. After baths and teeth had been seen to, there on the bottom of Geordie's bed were the clothes his Mam had bought for him, including the new shoes. He picked them up in a daze. Cockney's sharp voice brought him back to reality.

'The sooner you're in bed asleep Geordie, the quicker you'll be on that bus goin home.'

He knew his mate was right. After Sister came around with their medication and everyone had knelt for their bedside prayers, it took a while for him to get to sleep. His mind was that active thinking of his Mam and home, but eventually he drifted off.

The following morning it was up, wash, brush teeth and dress. At first it felt a bit strange standing in his own clothes and not in the khaki shirt, shorts and plimsoles.

After breakfast, the kids who were going home sat on the edge of the benches, waiting for the bus to arrive. One of the boys looked out of the window and cried out, 'It's here. The bus is here.'

Everyone dashed toward the windows as the bus came down the narrow road. Shortly after, they climbed aboard as Sister checked each child on her list. Geordie and Cockney grabbed the two best seats at the back, away from Sister's watching eye. Geordie turned around to get a glimpse of the field from the bus and saw some boys standing on the edge of the tarmac. One, with his hands in his pockets, drew his attention. It was the boy who had gone hysterical on hearing that he would not be going home. He'd obviously been crying, as his face around his eyes was all red. Geordie gave Cockney a nudge with his elbow and nodded toward the boy. Cockney glanced through the window and said, 'Yeah, I saw him.'

As Sister climbed aboard she spoke to the driver and the bus drove off. Before they knew it they were pulling into Paddington Station. Every boy sat until his name was called out, he was then handed over to whoever was picking him up. Geordie's name was one of the first and as he walked down the bus Cockney shouted, 'See you Geordie.' He lifted his arm in acknowledgement.

He stepped down from the bus. At first, he did not recognise the man Sister was telling that it had taken a while for Geordie to settle in, but that he was adapting nicely to his surroundings and school. Then it all came back to him. That was Mr King, signing papers and looking down at him saying, 'Come on George, you'll be keen to get home I take it?'

'He had no idea,' thought Geordie.

CHAPTER 6

THIS TIME HIS eyes were all over the underground taking in everything he could see. His mates back home would have a field day if they lived here.

On the approach to Newcastle, Geordie stood in the train corridor, eyes fixed on the River Tyne. It looked dirtier than ever as the train slowly crossed the high-level bridge and shunted its way into the Newcastle Central Station. There on the platform was his Mam, he couldn't get off the train quick enough to get to her. When he did, he burst into tears and held on to her as tight as he could.

'Oh, we've missed you,' Mam told him as she cuddled him close to her. After Mam had spoken to Mr King, they walked out of the Central Station, crossed the busy road to the bus stop. Before long they were crossing the Tyne Bridge on the bus, then up the Gateshead High Street, where it turned left at the junction of Sunderland Road and the Empire Picture House. They got off the bus outside the Hykey Park. He could not help but look at it. Nothing had changed while he'd been away. Three swings, a roundabout, and that was it. But he was glad he was looking at it and not just thinking about it.

It seemed strange walking into his back lane and yard with its outside toilets. His Mam knew he was thinking about what he had written, telling her all about Chalfont Colony, where there was no rubbish anywhere in sight, roads were swept on a regular basis, everything was big, the houses and well-kept gardens, the teeth brushing morning and night, prayers at every meal and bedtime, attending church every Sunday and, worst of all, bed at six o'clock every night.

She told him, 'Don't worry. It'll all come back to you, you'll see.'

His brothers and sisters were full of questions, which he did his best to answer. After tea Mam told him to change out of his good clothes and shoes and she would iron them and put them away. In the bedroom he forgot for a moment that he was getting changed to go out and play and not to go to bed, then a shout came up the back stairs, 'MRS HARBORN, IS YOR GEORDIE BACK YIT.'

It was his mate who lived next door.

Mam shouted back, 'He is. He'll not be lang.'

As he headed out the kitchen door Mam told his mate, 'He's just got back, so don't get into any trouble.'

Geordie gave her a smile and closed the door behind him. His mates were full of questions, which he soon got sick of answering. But it was good to hear them speaking broad Geordie instead of the King's English.

'Whey, how lang yi yem for like?'

'Don't know. Think it's for the summer holidays.'

'Whey ya ta-kin a bit funny Geordie like.'

'How'd you mean?'

'Weel, like funny, like yi nau what a mean, like posh tark.'

'Aw, that's cos of the kids I've been with. They come from all over the country man.'

'Ah weel, that'll not last lang.'

Geordie told them about running away but getting caught by the coppers. When they asked how far he'd got, he stretched it to, 'Just outside London.'

Then he told them all about the London underground, with the stairs that moved on their own.

'How many stairs wor there then?'

'Aw, there must be aboot fifty or sixty stairs ganning up and doon. In they never stop.'

After kicking the ball around for a while, it was time to go back in. Geordie's eyes were starting to close on him, it had been a long time since he'd been up this late.

As they said goodnight one of his mates asked, 'So have they cured yi of ya fits then?'

'Nah, am still taking them.'

'Well what's the point of ganning there then?'

'Ah divint nah, diva ye tell me?'

That summer was one of the best holidays in his life. He felt the freedom of being able to do anything without having to look around to see Sister Tate watching him. He soon settled back home again, as his Mam had said. He did his best to keep out of trouble, thinking if he behaved himself Mam might keep him at home. Geordie was still taking fits, but at least his mates were used to seeing it happen and took no notice. If they were playing football and he took one they would just shout out, 'Hold it, wait till he's finished.' A few minutes later they'd be shouting, 'Right that's it, was wor ball', only for a big argument to start.

When they ended up on the Gateshead High Street one of his mates told him, if he got caught nicking out of one of the shops they might not take him back to the special school.

'What, you want me to get caught?' Geordie asked.

'Well, let's face it Geordie, not even yee can be in two places at once can yi?'

'Ah divint nah what yi meen,' he replied.

'Well, if yi got caught yid have ti gan ti court, so yi'd not have ti gan away agin to the special school. Yi cannit dee both can yi?'

'Oh aye, ind a could end up ganning ti somewhere worse as well. Piss off with ya stupid idea's will yi.'

By the end of the holidays he had lost the bit of King's English he had gained – it was the old saying, you are the company you keep. Given the choice, Geordie would have gone for home any time.

It was nearing the end of the holidays and all the kids were talking about, including Geordie, was going to see *King Kong* at the Empire Picture House the next week. But then his Mam told him that everyone was back at school on Monday and he'd be at Chalfont Colony. He was so disappointed. His Mam did her best to explain to him why he had to go back – and in the nicest possible way. In turn, he tried to convince her to keep him at home by telling her loads of things to try. She told him he would be home for Christmas, which wasn't that far off. He felt sick to his stomach just thinking about it.

So, his mates would get to see *King Kong* but without him. He'd be back in khaki uniform with Sister Tate. This only made him feel bitter about the place.

~

Monday morning came around too soon. Geordie and his Mam were on the bus once more, heading for the Central Station in Newcastle. At the end of Sunderland Road a large poster of *King Kong* was on the Empire's walls. Mam knew how disappointed he was and gave him a hug with her left arm.

At the train station he poured his heart out, begging his Mam not to send him back again. It was a struggle for her to let go, she knew when he really meant something, and this was no acting on his part. As the train pulled away, he watched his Mam fade out of sight. Had one of the doors been open he would have jumped from the train with no regard to his safety. That's how desperate he was at that moment in his young life.

Most of the way down to King's Cross there was little conversation between him and Mr King. Although Mr King asked him questions about his holidays, which only depressed him even more. He did tell him about the boy who didn't go home for his holidays and wondered what had happened to him. But he felt that Mr King didn't quite believe what he was telling him, so they sat in silence for most of the journey.

The novelty of the underground and going up and down the elevators had worn off. It was just like home really, only they used buses to get to work not an underground railway. When they came up out of the underground at Paddington Station the first thing that caught his eye were the two buses surrounded by parents and kids. The boys' bus with Sister Tate was at the rear, the girls' bus was some distance away. Mr King wasn't taking any chances with Geordie, who was fast and nimble on his feet, and did as his Mam had told him, to make sure to keep tight hold of him. Until he handed him over to Sister Tate, George was his responsibility.

'That's us George, over there,' he indicated with his free hand.

As they approached the bus Sister Tate stepped forward, 'Ah yes, Mr King isn't it, with George.'

She ushered Geordie on board the bus without giving Mr King any time for a last word. Nevertheless, Mr King, being the gentleman that he was, took time to make sure that Geordie was settled on the bus and gave him a wave before turning and heading straight back into the underground. Geordie plonked himself in a window seat overlooking the station to watch all the activity going on outside. He cheered up when he saw Cockney climb on board with a face like a ripe tomato.

'What the hell happened to you,' he asked as Cockney sat himself down next to him.

'How'd you mean?'

'Well yor face, it's all red.'

'We spent the last three weeks at my grandma's down in Brighton. It was fuckin red hot down there. Spent most of the time on the beach. Did you go anywhere for the holidays?'

'I did, I went home,' Geordie replied.

'I know you went fuckin home. But did you go anywhere else is what I'm askin.'

'Nah. Me granny only lives a few streets away from us. Far as ah got was wor back lane.'

What his mates had said kept running through his head, 'Well if it was us nowt would stop us from deeing a bunk.'

He told Cockney that he was supposed to be going to see *King Kong* this week with his mates. Cockney told him he'd seen it. In fact, he'd seen it twice and it was great. Not to worry, he'd tell him all about it. This depressed Geordie more than ever. He stood up and squeezed past Cockney, telling him he'd had enough of this lot, he was heading back home to see *King Kong* with his mates. Cockney told him not to be stupid; he was in the middle of fucking London, hundreds of miles from home, and if he got lost in this place, he'd know about it.

'Then I won't get lost fucking lost, will I?' Geordie answered.

Cockney did his best to try and get him to sit back down and see sense.

'Listen Geordie, I know London better than you. It's a hell of a big place and I'm tellin you, kids go missin every week and are never heard of again. Take my kiddin, don't even think about it … you listenin to me or what?'

Geordie's head was elsewhere with home firmly stamped in his mind. Cockney did his best to talk him out of it.

'She'll see you gettin off the fuckin bus, don't be daft!' Cockney whispered not wanting other kids to know what was going on.

Geordie walked to the front with his eyes glued on Sister Tate, who had her back toward the entrance to the bus. The driver was busy loading suitcases into the luggage compartment. He took his chance and stepped down, only a few feet from Sister Tate. His heart was beating that loud he felt sure she would hear it. Quickly, he nipped round the front of the bus and down the other side of it, where there was nothing but a tall wall of the station. He was totally out of sight of everyone except Cockney, who was watching his every move and trying to keep his eye on Sister Tate at the same time.

'The minute he walks out from the bus she's goin to spot him,' thought Cockney, who was now feeling the anxiety more than Geordie.

Geordie stood to the rear of the bus, trying to decide which way to walk without being seen and caught by her. Should he try and walk out the station when a small crowd came up from the underground heading for the exit, or try walking across the station toward the underground in the hope she would be too busy to notice him? Cockney was watching his every move and knew what his mate was thinking.

'Oh Geordie, you're in deep shit me bonnie lad. The minute you step out she'll spot you, then all hell will let loose.'

At that moment two boys came down the aisle of the bus to sit in the back seats. Cockney turned and looked at them, 'Fuck off, these seats are taken.' The last thing he wanted was a load of kids staring out at what was going on.

Geordie popped his head around the back of the bus to check which way Sister was standing. By this time most of the kids were on the bus so there was less of a crowd to hide behind. Taking his chance he made his move. Cockney was expecting him to either go across the open station or toward the exit up the slight incline then out the station, but Geordie thought, 'She's going to spot me. Cockney's right,' so he walked away from the bus, still out of sight of Sister, toward the rubbish bin. He then bent down behind it, pretending to fasten his shoelaces. Cockney moaned to himself, 'Oh Geordie,' thinking he was going to hide behind a bin, and then watched in disbelief as Geordie opened the lid of the bin and jumped inside. In the blink of an eye he was totally out of sight. Cockney sat back down, laughing away to himself, 'Only a fuckin Geordie would have thought of that.' If he hadn't seen it with his own eyes he would never have believed it. 'Now the fun will start when she finds out he's not on the bus.'

Then he realised that she was going to blame him for helping his mate get of the bus. He could be in deep shit. It was as well that nobody had taken the slightest bit notice of what had been going on around them. Then he thought, she's bound to ask me about him, so he tried to think of something to keep himself in the clear. Sister stepped on board the bus with her papers and her checklist. 'Hell, here we go,' he thought, crouching down into his seat.

'Silence everyone,' Sister Tate called out. 'For any new boys, first time with us, my name is Sister Tate, not nurse, not miss, but Sister Tate. And that is how you will address me if you have anything to say, do you understand me?'

A handful muttered, 'Yes Sister.'

'Good. I shall now take a head count to make sure we haven't left anyone behind. Answer yes or present when you hear your name.'

As she started her head count an idea dawned on Cockney. He stood up and interrupted the count.

'Excuse me, Sister.'

'You should know better than to interrupt me while I'm busy. What is it boy?'

'I only wanted to know if George was coming back?'

For a few moments she didn't speak, then she asked abruptly what he meant by that question.

'I was just wonderin if he might be comin later, with him not bein here.'

Sister hurried down the aisle, checking each seat as she went toward the back of the bus. She then turned to Cockney and bent close to his face, 'Where is he then? Come on, I know you'll be part of this. Where is he?'

'Sister, he wasn't on the bus when I got on, honest. He wasn't. I've never seen him.'

The two buses were held up, while the Sisters searched all over the station. They notified the station police, but to no avail. Cockney watched their every move. Sister went toward a police officer who was approaching the bus from the rear. The two were only a few feet from the bin where Geordie was holding his nose because of the smell. They only had to put something in the bin, and he would be caught out. After quite a long time Sister climbed back on the bus. Her face was nearly the same colour as Cockney's. She walked straight toward him.

'Last chance. Where is he?' her nose was nearly touching Cockney's.

'He wasn't on the bus when I got on it Sister. I've already told you.'

Standing at the front of the bus she clapped her hands, 'Silence everyone. I want to ask you all something particularly important.' She paused, 'Did any of you see a boy getting back off the bus? Now think very carefully, this is important.'

Cockney got the fright of his life when one of the new boys put his hand in the air. 'Shit,' he thought, 'did he see the two of them sitting together?'

She dashed to where the boy was sitting, 'Yes, yes. What did you see my boy. Did you see him get off the bus then?'

The boy was beginning to wish he'd never put his hand up. By now sister was right into the boy's face, practically spitting on him.

'Did you or did you not see him getting off the bus then boy?'

The youngster was petrified by his first taste of Sister at first hand.

'I didn't see him getting off, I saw him getting on.'

Straight away sister was in for the kill, 'And who did he sit down next to?' she glanced at Cockney.

'I'll fuckin kill the little bastard if he says me,' thought Cockney.

'He was sitting on his own,' he told her.

Sister rolled her eyes to the sky and groaned and then the young lad added, 'And then I looked out the window and saw him walking away with a man. I thought it was his dad, miss.'

For a moment Cockney thought Sister was going to have a fit when she heard Geordie had walked off with a total stranger. He knew straight away the boy had made the whole thing up to try and look good in front of everyone. He had no idea of the kind of trouble he'd got himself into as he did his best to try and get out of what he'd just told her.

'And what did this man look like? Answer me boy when I speak to you.'

By now the boy was practically in tears, 'I don't know miss. I only saw their backs as they walked away.'

Sister stared at the boy as she said, 'And my name is Sister Tate, and don't you forget it boy.'

The bus was a good hour late pulling out of Paddington Station. Sister Tate had to get back off the bus to make some phone calls. She had scoured the inside and the outside of the station looking for Geordie. Twice she had stood right next to the bin with one of the police officers. On one occasion she was heard telling the officer that he was a very bright child but he was 300 miles from home. The officer was concerned for him, especially when he heard that someone had walked away with him as London was an extremely dangerous place for kids, especially after dark. Geordie was in two minds about jumping out of the bin there and then as his legs started to cramp. But he stayed in the bin and eventually watched the bus pull out of the station with a very worried Sister on board. This had never happened to her before and, although she was strict, she was genuinely very concerned about Geordie. One thing he did know, that Sister Tate would never forget him, even if she never saw him again.

Cockney took one last look at the bin as they pulled away. Even he wasn't sure if he'd done the right thing in leaving him there to try and get himself home with nothing but the clothes he stood in.

After watching the bus pull out of the station Geordie sat for a while peeping out from under the lid. It all looked clear, with no police hanging about, so out he jumped. He was as stiff as a poker and stretched his legs and back, trying to decide which way to go. If he headed down the underground there could be police looking for him. He glanced at the exit up the slight incline, which would take him out of the station, 'That's it. I'll give it a few hours to make sure there's no coppers hanging around in the underground.' Dusting himself down he headed up the incline and out of the station on to the main road and pavement.

'Wow this place is busy,' he told himself as he looked up at all the buildings and traffic. 'You could get lost here, no bother.'

He told himself that he'd better watch where he was going, or else he'd never find his way back to the station and underground. All sorts ran through his mind. Sister Tate would never remember what he was wearing, so they would have to get in touch with his Mam to find out, then his Mam will be worried about him, his Dad would hit the ceiling when he heard about it. Then on top of it all he might have got his Mam in trouble. He turned and walked up a few streets, there were shops everywhere you looked; he couldn't see any houses anywhere.

All this time he kept his eyes open for any coppers. After walking for a while, he turned up into what looked like a quiet street, away from all the big fancy shops and buildings. There were only a few small shops and what looked to him like a café. It was like one he'd been in with his Mam a long time ago. It was on the corner of a building, a grotty looking place, more for working men and down and outs or, in his mind, tramps. He would feel safer there than in one of the big shops, who he knew always had people looking out for kids on their own trying to shop lift, that was no good to him.

He stood in the middle of the pokey shop looking at the glass counter with a few scones and cakes behind it. The fat man behind the counter asked him, 'Well, do you want anything or what?'

'Glass of pop and a chocolate biscuit,' Geordie replied.

The fat man placed them on top of the glass counter. Geordie handed over the half-crown his Mam had given him that morning. Geordie didn't move as he stood waiting for his change, hand held out. If the place had been empty there would have been no chance of getting his change, only for the fact that three workmen sitting getting their break had watched the transaction. The fat man placed his change on the glass counter. Geordie picked it up and sat himself at one of the few tables scattered about the place, it was next to the window which allowed him to look up and down the street. There were two elderly women sitting in the corner he hadn't noticed when he came in. One of them smiled at him as he sat down. He was doing his best to remember his way back to the station.

The man behind the counter kept looking across at him until eventually he asked, 'You waiting for someone sonny?'

Doing his best to cover his accent, he told him his mam was in the shops and told him to stay here until she got back for him. The man behind the counter frowned with suspicion. After another ten minutes of sitting looking up and down the street, Geordie began to feel uneasy, so he drank the last of his pop, stood up and walked toward the door.

'Thought you had to wait for your mam?' the fat man called out.

'I know where she'll be, I'll go and meet her.'

'Have another pop, it's on the house,' the man tired to tempt him to stay longer.

'Er, no thanks,' Geordie replied, as he hurried out the door and down the street. But he'd lost his sense of direction and didn't know which way to go.

At the bottom of the street he looked back to see the fat man watching him. The place was that big he was beginning to think that Cockney was right about London and kids never being heard of again. It wouldn't be long before it was dark, then what would he do?

~

When the bus arrived at Chalfont Colony there was no singing to be heard from any of the kids. A very worried Sister Tate got off the bus, spoke to Mr Hopwood, then vanished back up the road. Probably to report about one of the boys seeing him walk away from the bus and out of the station with a male stranger.

~

Geordie had ended up in a quiet backstreet with a few small shops, some of them were closing. Some of the taller buildings looked like grotty flats, with loads of dirty windows, some had net curtains that made them look worse. He was starting to wish he was back at Tate House. He wasn't feeling well, he was stressed out and lonely, and his sensations were starting in his thighs and arms. Silent tears came from his eyes as he sat himself down in one of the empty shop doorways, started fitting and blanked out.

~

Back home it was nearly seven o'clock when a loud rap came on his Mam's front door. His Dad was getting ready to go out for a pint.

'Who the hell's that at the front door?' he said, looking at Mam.

'I don't know but yi better frigging answer it before they knock the door doon,' she told him.

Dad hurried down the stairs shouting, 'All reet, I'm coming.' There in front of him were two big coppers. Dad looked at them, 'I think you've got the wrong door this time,' he said, with young Geordie in mind.

'Can we come in for a moment?' one asked.

'Aye a suppose so.' He pointed at the gas metre halfway up the stairs. 'Watch ya heed on the metre when yi come up.'

They followed him up the bare wooden stairs, ducked their heads halfway up to miss the metre, and went into the kitchen. Mam was shocked to see two policemen.

'Well, what's it all aboot? Has one of them done someick rang?' Dad asked, referring to the kids.

The older policeman said, 'No, it's nothing of that nature that we've come to see you about.'

The other officer turned to Mam and told her maybe she should sit down to hear what they had to tell her.

'Why what is it what's happened?' she asked as she sat down on the settee.

The kids were still playing outside – had one of them done something wrong?

'It's about your young lad, George,' said the older officer.

'Well HE couldn't have done owt rang, he's away in a special school. In fact, he only went this morning,' said Dad straight away.

'That's what we've come to see you about.'

'Oh my God, some-icks happened to him hasn't there. Is he all right?' Mam asked with a sharp intake of breath and hand over her mouth.

'That's the problem that we have. You see we don't know if he's all right or not at the moment,' replied the older officer.

'I knew it. Oh my God, he's had an accident.' Mam was beside herself with worry not being there for him.

The officer went on to tell them that they knew their laddie was in a home for epileptics and that was what they had come to see them about.

'Has he done owt rang or has he …' Dad was interrupted by the other officer who went on to explain that Geordie had been placed on the bus with the other kids at Paddington

Station in London, but when the person in charge made a head count of the children she discovered their laddie was missing.

Dad looked at the clock, 'Hang on. What time did he go missing?'

'We haven't got the exact time but from what we know it would be some time around one o'clock.'

'And he's still missing? It's frigging seven a clock at neet and they still haven't fund him?'

'The Metropolitan police are on the lookout for him. They are aware of his medical condition.'

It hadn't taken long for the neighbours to notice the police at Geordie's home. One of his brothers came into the kitchen, 'Cannit be for that Geordie. He's already away. Wonder who it's for then?'

The brother was soon followed by his older sister, more curious than anything else. Dad chased them into the bedroom, where they stood listening what was being said.

'He might be alreet pet. The London police will be right on top of this. They'll find him, don't worry,' said Dad, trying his best to calm Mam down.

Mam shouted out, 'He's only a bairn. Nee money, nee medication. Lost somewhere in London. I wish to God we'd never sent him in the forst place.' She broke down, crying her eyes out.

His sister came out of the bedroom and placed her arms around her. It was rare to see Mam crying at anything.

The two officers felt rather awkward and told Dad that if they heard anything at all they would let them know immediately. When they had gone the family sat, saying nothing for a while.

'Eeh, if owt happens to him I'll never forgive me sell for letting him gan in the forst place,' Mam cried.

'Divint be daft woman. He's got a heed on his shoulders. He's not stupid. He'll be all reet. Yill see.'

Mam sat shaking, her head in her hands. She looked up at Dad, 'Are yee stupid or what? Even yee couldn't git from the middle of London with nee money or owt else, never mind a bairn like him.'

Dad knew there was no answer to that. He simply sat in his old armchair, clutching his hands tightly until his knuckles turned white.

There was a heavy knocking at the front door.

'Sit there, I'll get it.' Dad hurried down the front stairs and there stood the neighbour from next door.

'Is everything alreet? it's just that a saw the police at ya door at this time of neet?'

'Yi best come up Bella. She's upstairs.'

Bella hurried up the stairs and into the kitchen. Mam was sobbing. Bella put her arm around her, trying to comfort her by saying, 'Haway now, it'll be alreet.'

'Young Geordie's went missing somewhere in London,' Dad told her.

'Diven't worry pet. I'm sure they'll find him.'

'That's what I've told her,' said Dad.

When Bella had gone, Geordie's older sister Betty entered the room, 'I wouldn't worry aboot him Mam. He can look after hisself.'

'I hope so love. Now get yourselves back to bed,' Mam said with a heavy sigh.

Dad knew he wasn't doing any good just sitting on top of Mam, so he got himself up out of his chair and decided to go for a pint rather than not knowing what to say for the best. He had only been in his regular bar for an hour when one of the neighbours walked in. After getting himself a pint, he sat down next to him.

'Is that right what they're all talking aboot Geordie? Aboot yor young un ganning missing somewhere in London?'

'Aye it's reet enough Jimmy. Addlike ti nah where the frigging hell he is.'

'Yor lass must be worried sick aboot im.'

'Yi divint nah the half of it. She's sitting there worrying a-sell ti death aboot im.'

'How the hell did it happen?' Jimmy asked.

'Ah divint nah. All wi nah is, he was put on a bus with some other kids, when they came ti check them all he was missing.'

'Well al tell yi what somebody wants, it's a foot up tha arses for ti let that happen,' he told Dad.

'A nah, he was always in trouble ind all that, but he doesn't deserve owt like this happening ti him,' replied Dad as he swigged back his pint.

Mam was still sitting when Dad came back.

'Haway lets get ti bed, it's nee good sitting up al neet. They'll let wi nah if they git any news aboot im,' said Dad.

'Aye, it's what kind of news that am worried aboot.'

~

Geordie was sitting in the shop doorway, coming out of his fit, as he made out a figure coming toward him. His vision started to clear and he saw what looked like some kind of tramp, now standing over him.

'You okay kid?' He asked as he bent right over him. 'Come on you, come wif me and I'll take you where you can sleep for the night.' He put his grubby arms around him and lifted him to his feet. He took a quick look around and tried to rush him down one of the back alleys full of bins and rubbish.

Geordie wasn't well, the sensations were all over him, he felt dizzy, plus the man smelt of fish.

Out of nowhere a woman's voice shouted, 'OY YOU'. the man turned and saw the woman running toward them. 'YER YOU GET YER BLEEDIN ANDS OFF IM YI DIRTY PERVERT.'

He took one look at her, dropped his hold of Geordie and went belting up one of the side alleys out of sight.

'You all right me old cock? Didn't touch you or anyfin did eh? The dirty barstered. We all know what he is, the dirty pervert.'

The woman was nothing like his Mam. She was wearing bright red lipstick, high heels and fancy stockings, plus she smelt a bit like a sweet shop.

'Never seen you round these quarters before. You're definitely not from around here sonny. So where are you from then? Where you livin?'

'Newcastle,' he replied, he'd learnt long before that no one knew where Gateshead was.

'Bleedin ell! You're a long way from Newcastle sonny. So, ow cum you're on your own then?'

'Got lost from me mam at the railway station.'

'What station would that be then? There's lots of stations round London sonny.'

'Paddington, it's Paddington Station. Me mam won't leave without me. She'll stay at the station looking for me.'

'Come on sonny, it's your lucky bleedin day. I'm going that way, it just so appens it's on my patch.'

As they headed toward the station, Geordie noticed she kept looking all over the place – he couldn't help but think she might just be on the lookout for a copper. He was relieved when the station came in sight. As they went down the ramp, he could see it wasn't as busy as when he'd left it.

They were standing next to a ticket machine and he knew it was happening once again. The woman looked down at him, asking could he see his mum anywhere, but before he could answer he fell to his knees taking another fit. When he came around out of it, he was sitting with his back against the machine with two women looking down at him plus the woman who had helped him find the station. She asked him if he was all right, 'What just appened? You scared the bleedin daylights out of me. You stay where you are while I go and speak to somebody. Now don't you move, you hear me?'

As she spoke she brushed his hair out of his face with her long, painted fingernails. This woman was kind, but she was nothing like his Mam. He sat and watched her walk across the station in her high-heel shoes and fancy stockings into the office. This wasn't looking good, he had to make himself scarce and quick, even though the woman had been kind enough to help him. He stood up, helped by the other two women, then high-tailed it across the station into a crowd. He ran down one escalator, on to the platform and jumped in the first train that came rolling into the station from one of the tunnels. He didn't have a clue where it was heading. Looking up, he saw the first station that it stopped at, he saw the station name on the train that told him each station it stopped at. Nowhere could he see the name King's Cross. He was travelling in the wrong direction he was moving further away from King's Cross, going deeper into London. He jumped off the train at the first chance he got and walked over to the opposite platform where he jumped on the first train going the other way. Even then he wasn't sure if he was doing the right thing.

CHAPTER 7

AT CHALFONT COLONY everyone had been talking about Geordie going missing in London. Word soon spread from Tate House to the Princess of Wales girls' house next door. Every boy on the bus had been questioned more than once. Even the girls were asked if they had noticed a boy walking away from the bus, either on his own or with someone. They ended up with all kinds of tales, which was no help at all.

The boy who had told Sister Tate that he'd seen a boy walking away with a man, was now saying that he could have been mistaken.

Cockney had been questioned the most, especially by Sister Tate. He kept telling her the same story, that Geordie wasn't on the bus when he got on and that's why he'd asked her, 'Was George not coming back this year?' The only worry Cockney had was if his mate did come back and he mentioned he was sitting next to him he would really be in deep shit. Sister had checked her log roll and knew that Cockney had boarded the bus after George, so there was the possibility that Cockney was telling the truth. But she still had a suspicion he was involved in some way or another. That night, when he climbed into bed, he looked over to his mate's empty bed and asked, 'Where the fuckin hell are you Geordie?'

Sister Tate was concerned about one of her wards going missing while in her charge, but she was more concerned about his safety than anything else. Cockney couldn't imagine her getting much sleep that night.

~

Back in the underground, Geordie was now wondering where the hell he was. He knew he was going to have to ask someone for directions, but who? That was the question. There were only a few people on the train, sitting in the far corner was an old woman, in the other direction a crowd of drunks were celebrating something, and there was a young lad, probably five or six year older than himself. Taking the chance, he walked toward the young lad and sat in the next seat to him. The lad gave him a glance and that was all. In his best voice Geordie asked if he could direct him to King's Cross Station. The lad never answered. Geordie asked again.

The lad looked at him, 'Where you from them?'

Geordie said Newcastle and asked his question again.

The lad stared at him then asked, 'You on the run then?'

Geordie didn't know what to answer but he needn't have worried as the lad went on, 'Second thoughts, don't tell me. I don't want to know.' He got up and as he went toward the opening doors he pointed to the board up on the train wall, 'You've got four more stops. Get off, then go up the escalators, cross the road, and that's King's Cross.' As the doors started to close, he gave a shout, 'GOOD LUCK MATE, AND WATCH FOR THE GUARDS.' Then he was gone.

Geordie sat there looking out at every station and counting off each one in turn. At the fourth he jumped off the tube and headed for the escalator. At the top he looked around for the exit. Once outside, he saw the station across the main road. At last, he'd found it! He was still a long way from home but in his head he could hear his mates in the back lane telling him he could do it – plus, he wanted to see *King Kong* at the Empire.

Inside King's Cross there were huge numbers of people walking around. No one took the slightest notice of him being on his own. Everyone was busy with themselves, hurrying back and forth all over the place. The station was different to the one in Newcastle, it was far bigger and it even had shops inside. There were six or seven platforms in a row with trains standing at the side of them. You had to go through a turnstile, showing your ticket to be able to get through any one of them. Question was, how was he going to manage to get past one of them. And, even if he managed it, what train must he get on to take him to Newcastle? After wandering around looking for some way to get on a platform, he spotted the mail bags all stacked up on their trollies. There were even some empty pigeon baskets standing nearby and some steel boxes near them. They were all on the other side of steel barriers that were too high to climb, as he'd be spotted going over them. He walked right to the end of the steel rails and looked at the gap in the last rail, it was slightly wider than the rest of the rails. Could he squeeze through? Geordie gave a quick look around, dropped to his knees and placed his head through the end gap. Yes, his head went through. Slowly he squeezed his slim body through the rails and before he knew it he was on the other side. He casually walked away from the mail bags and along to where all the trains were standing, he still hadn't a clue which train he should jump on. He had no idea what all the writing was about, flashing up on all the boards in the station. Two of the trains had closed all their doors and were preparing to move out of the station. If one of them were going to Newcastle it was too late. He was beginning to wonder if any of them was the train he wanted to get back home. He could hear the lady on the loudspeaker telling people the platform number and each train's destination. He couldn't quite understand what she was saying. He did hear her mention different cities and was beginning to wonder if he should take a chance and jump on a train. At least it would get him to somewhere they weren't looking for him. Moments later he heard the lady mention Newcastle in her cockney accent. Geordie's ears pricked up closely listening to what she was saying as she repeated her message once again. He heard the words York, Durham, then Newcastle, followed by Edinburgh, what he couldn't make out was which platform the train was on. He had a choice. There were six trains standing, with two of them getting ready to pull out of the station. Then he spotted a guard coming his way. He decided rather than getting caught now he'd take his chance and jump on the nearest train. Once out of sight of the guard he felt more at ease, until he heard the slamming of the doors on the train he'd jumped on. Too late for him to get off, plus the fact that the guard would see him. The train slowly moved out of the station.

'What the hell,' he thought, 'at least it'll take me out of London.' Trouble was, he just didn't know where to. First thing he learnt was to get out of sight by diving into the nearest toilet. He seemed to be sitting on the toilet seat for ages as he listened to people talking as they passed by. A couple tried the door to see if it was occupied. When that happened, rather than saying anything out loud, he would give a deep cough, which usually did the trick.

Once the train was moving at full speed, he took himself out of the toilets and walked along the corridors, glancing into each carriage to see if and where he thought was a safe place to sit himself down.

'This'll do,' he thought, as he investigated one of the carriages where an elderly woman was sitting on her own next to the window. On the opposite side an older guy was sitting tucked in the corner next to the door reading a newspaper. He slid the door open and sat himself down opposite the elderly lady, who gave him a glance then continued looking out of the window. The man in the other corner never gave him a second look and simply carried on reading his newspaper. The lady turned her head and eyed him up and down. Geordie gave her a quick smile in acknowledgement. He was shattered after everything he'd been through and before he knew it he was asleep in his seat. The lady in the corner tried to figure out what he was doing travelling on his own.

The clashing of the carriage doors woke him up to the voice of the conductor calling out, 'TICKETS PLEASE.'

He knew he had to get out of sight. But where? Doing his best to keep calm he got to his feet, stretched his arms and casually strolled out of the carriage and into the passageway. Once out of sight he hurried away from the conductor's direction, looking for somewhere to hide until the danger was gone. He'd gone as far as he could, with nowhere but the toilet left. He went in and didn't know whether to lock the door or not. If he was home what would he do? He squeezed down on the floor below the washbasin and behind the door, making himself into as small a ball as he could. He deliberately left the door open. Minutes later he could hear the conductor in the corridor next to the toilet. He didn't feel well with all the anxiety and stress. 'I'm not taking a fit,' he kept on telling himself, when suddenly the toilet door opened right up to his knees, which he was keeping tight hold of. The toilet door closed abruptly. Geordie gave a sigh of relief and a few minutes later he was in the middle of a fit and blanked out.

~

The following morning Cockney woke up, half-expecting to see his Geordie mate in the bed across him. No such joy. 'Oh, shit Geordie. Where the hell are you?' He lay on his back staring at his mate's empty bed with all kinds of things going through his head. He lived in Camden Town and had been warned dozens of times by his family about kids going missing in London and never heard of or seen again in England's main city. He was starting to feel guilty about his mate who had never been outside of Paddington Station. He knew even his chances were slim if he'd spent the night on London streets, especially with no money or medication. Someone would pick him up, the question was … who?

At breakfast that morning Cockney noticed Sister Tate was unusually quiet. The suspense was killing him. As he walked out of the door to go to school he stopped right in front of her, 'Excuse me Sister, have you had any word about George please?'

She looked down at him with a blank face, 'No, we have had no word.'

This answer made Cockney even more worried. Maybe he should have told someone about him hiding in the bin, If anything had happened to Geordie, he had two choices: one, to keep stum; two, place himself right in deep shit and who knows what else. He did know that if anything happened to his Geordie mate and they found out he was involved in him going missing, then he would really be in massive trouble.

~

It wasn't long before the motion of the train rocked Geordie to sleep once again. He didn't know how long he'd been asleep. Again, it was the clashing of the doors that woke him. Still drowsy he knew the train was pulling into a station and he also knew he would have to take the chance and try to see where he was, he could be anywhere in the country. He looked outside the carriage window and could just make out a sign saying York. He could have jumped for joy. He didn't know how far York was from Newcastle, but he did know that Durham was usually after York, and the next stop after Durham had to be Newcastle.

He dived back into the toilets remembering to leave the door open for the benefit of the conductor. Once the train was picking up speed, he made his way back to one of the carriages. Then he didn't feel well and dropped back down to the floor, taking another fit. When he came around he was pleased to see he was still on his own, but he felt terrible, shattered and exhausted. After a drink of water from the washbasin he made his way to one of the carriages and sat himself down. Then he realised he was in the same carriage that he had got into at King's Cross, with the same lady sitting in the corner window seat.

The lady recognised him immediately and wondered why anyone so young would be travelling so far on his own. After a while she was unable to contain her curiosity and asked him politely, 'Did I not see you getting on the train at King's Cross?'

Geordie's little brain started racing nineteen to the dozen, not wanting to give himself away at this stage of the game. 'Er, yes, I think so,' he stuttered.

'You think so?' she replied with a frown.

'Sorry. I meant, yes you did,' he replied in his best English. 'Are you travelling on your own?'

'Yes,' and nodded his head confidently.

'You look a bit young to be travelling on your own. Where are you travelling to then, if you don't mind me asking?'

'I'm travelling to Newcastle. Me mam is meeting me at the Central Station. She'll be waiting for me when I get there,' he told her with growing confidence, knowing he wasn't far from Newcastle.

'Oh, I see. Have you been away for the summer holidays then?'

He didn't like all these questions but had no choice than to go along with them. His little brain racing, trying to anticipate the way she was going with these questions.

'Yes, I've been staying at my cousins. I go there every summer.'

There was no hesitation in his voice. Geordie could be a convincing liar when he wanted to be.

'Ah, and now it's time to go back to school, eh?' She winked as if she had discovered his secret.

'Hmm,' he agreed, shaking of his head as if he regretted the holidays were over.

'Never mind, you've always got Christmas to look forward to.'

Again, he just nodded his head in agreement. After a slight pause in the conversation the lady asked, 'Do your cousins live in London then?'

These questions were getting a bit to near the mark for Geordie, but he was still on the ball and answered, hoping that was the last of the questions, 'No, they live in Buckinghamshire.'

'Oh, that's a lovely part of the country, what part of Buckinghamshire do they live in?'

'They live in Chalfont St Peter,' doing his best to end the questioning.

'Well, they live in a nice part of the county, I must say.'

Again, he only nodded his head in agreement.

She bent over and picked up a bag containing sandwiches. She asked if he would like one. Hhe didn't need to be asked twice, the last time he'd eaten was in the dirty old café and that was only a biscuit.

'Thank you,' he said politely.

She could tell he was hungry by the way he scoffed it down and offeredg him another. He didn't hesitate.

'Didn't your aunty put some sandwiches up for your journey home?' she asked.

'Yes, but I left them on the seat waiting for the train. My aunt will be cross about it.'

That seemed to be the end of the questioning and he gently fell asleep. The elderly lady drifted off to sleep herself as the train sped toward Newcastle and home. For some reason, the train didn't stop at Durham, the next stop was Newcastle Central Station.

Halfway between York and Newcastle Geordie heard the conductor checking tickets in the next carriage to them. He could see him in the passageway, no way was it possible to get out of his sight. The elderly lady was fast asleep, with her head against a small pillow. He knew this was a first-class carriage he was in and he had no other choice but to place his head against the side of the seat, close his eyes and pretend to be asleep. What else could he do? His heart was racing like the speeding train. He had come so far, only to be caught at the last hurdle! He did his best to think of some excuse. He must have lost his ticket. After all, from King's Cross his ticket had been checked twice, even the elderly lady would verify he had been with her since boarding the train. Hoping and praying it might work, eyes tight shut, he waited for the carriage door to slide open.

He heard the door of the carriage next to them close. This was it, he thought, getting ready to act his part. The conductor looked into the carriage and saw the elderly well-dressed lady asleep with what he thought could be her grandson, obviously too young to be travelling on his own. They were the only two in the first-class carriage. The conductor thought twice about disturbing them.

Geordie lay still for quite some time. He couldn't understand what was happening. Why hadn't the conductor opened their carriage door? Then he got up, slid open the door, looked up and down the passageway. Not a single person in it, he couldn't believe his luck. He sat himself back down and he fell asleep without having to worry about the conductor.

The train shuddered as it started to slow down, it was nearing Newcastle and he was still fast asleep. The elderly lady gently shook him as the train went over the Tyne.

'I think this is your stop,' she told him.

He was quickly wide awake and asked, 'Are you getting off here as well?' Knowing full well it was going to be awkward trying to get rid of her if she was.

'No, I'm travelling on to Edinburgh, but if you don't mind, can I ask, will you be able to get home from here?'

'Oh yes, me Mam will be …'

She stopped him in mid-sentence, 'Yes, I know what you told me about your mam meeting you. But tell me honestly, will you be able to get home all right from this station if she's not there for some reason?'

Geordie knew that somehow the elderly lady had sussed him out, but he wondered how.

'Oh yes, I can get home from here if me Mam's not here to meet me. With no bother at all. This is where I live.'

'Good,' she replied. 'I would be worried if you had any doubt about it. Oh, and by the way, the conductor looked in when we were both asleep. I think he didn't want to disturb us.'

He looked at her a bit puzzled. He wasn't thinking straight. He looked over the Tyne and saw the whole of Newcastle and Gateshead lit up. It was the best sight in the world. He was nearly home. When the train finally stopped, the lady opened the train door for him to get off, and called after him, 'Goodbye. Good luck. And be careful.'

He turned and gave her a little wave then walked toward a load of large bags stacked on top of one another. He was looking for a way out. It didn't take him long to spot what he was looking for. The barriers on Central Station were nowhere as high as the one in King's Cross. With it being very early morning there weren't many guards about as he quickly slid over the top and headed for the exit and out onto the streets of Newcastle. It gave him the feeling of being free, a feeling that was difficult to explain.

He knew that he still had to be careful. If he was spotted at that time in the morning he would be picked up by the police. It still wasn't quite daylight, but he had no choice other than to walk through the city streets, and then cross over the Tyne Bridge just as it was just turning light. He was knackered and tired and on top of all that he knew he needed his medication. The sensations were running wild in his mind and body, yet he kept on walking.

As he walked over the Tyne Bridge, he had to keep a keen eye out for cars and keet dodging behind the steel pillars of the bridge. Before long, he was at the end of the bridge and on Gateshead High Street. Using his head, he went up the back of the High Street, out of sight of anyone. He came to the end of Sunderland Road, facing the Empire, where he saw the giant poster for *King Kong*. The first person who came to his mind was Cockney, who was going to tell him all about the film, and who had told him, 'You'll never make it

Geordie. I live in London and you live fuckin near Scotland, hundreds of miles away.'

Yet here he was, walking along Sunderland Road. Even at this stage he kept to the back lanes until he came out the top of Railway Terrace and into the cobbles of Kirton Street. It was in darkness, apart from the corner gas lamp post. He was home at last. Standing in front of his own front door, for the first time he suddenly felt he could be in a lot of trouble with his Dad. He stood on his toes and reached up to the knocker on the front door, giving it three loud raps. At the same time he gave a quick look around, in case he'd woken any of the neighbours.

Mam sat bolt upright in bed before the third rap came on the door, giving Dad a dig with her elbow.

'There's somebody at the front door,' she cried out.

Dad jumped out of bed, putting his trousers on as quickly as he could. He hurried down the front stairs, expecting it to be police. He stood there speechless, looking at young Geordie in the semi-darkness.

All Geordie could say was, 'Sorry Dad.'

His Dad pulled him toward him and all he could say was, 'Christ All Mighty, get in'.

Mam got out of bed, nervous as hell, not knowing what or who to expect. At that time in the morning she was thinking it could only spell bad news. She heard Dad talking but couldn't make out what was said. She sat herself down in Dad's old chair, not knowing what kind of news she was about to get. She heard the footsteps coming up the wooden stairs. The door on the small landing at the top of the stairs leading into the kitchen was slightly open. Dad came in first.

'There's somebody here ti see yi Gort,' he said, as young Geordie popped his head from around Dad's back.

'Eh my God,' she cried out as she stood up and rushed to hold him. 'Where the hell have you been? We've been worried sick aboot yi.'

'I'm sorry Mam,' was all he could say.

'When was the last time yi had yor tablets?' Mam asked.

'Yesterday morning,' he replied.

She went straight to the cupboard to give him his medication she kept spare. Then she made him a large bowl of porridge with sugar in it. As he gulped it down him, Dad stood looking at him, shaking his head in disbelief.

'How the hell he's gitting from the middle of London all the way up here I divint nah, but there's a lot of people ganning ti git a shock when they find oot he's back yem on his own.'

'Aye well, let him get ti bed. He's had a lang day. We'll talk aboot it in the morning, alreet?' replied Mam.

Geordie climbed into bed in the middle of his brothers, where he felt safe and warm. His brothers just moaned about him getting in the middle. Mam told him she'd put another blanket on the bed. She came back into the bedroom with Dad's old topcoat and placed it over them. At last she could get some sleep herself, she thought as she climbed into bed and watched him while he fell asleep.

CHAPTER 8

WHEN HE FINALLY awoke it was mid-morning. After his breakfast Mam told him that he would have to go back. He asked her when. She told him it wouldn't be for a few days, possibly even next week. Meantime, she and Dad wanted to know how he had managed to get all the way back home on his own with only two and six in his pocket.

He told them everything, from the moment of getting off the bus, hiding inside the bin with Sister Tate not six feet away from him, his meeting the woman in London, to the train journey home. Mam asked if he had taken any fits on his way home. He told her he thought he had taken one in London, one in King's Cross, and two on the train.

She shook her head, uttering softly 'Oh my God.'

Later that day, Mam informed the police station that her son was back home. It wasn't long before there was another visitor knocking on her front door. Geordie wasn't sure who it was, but after the visitor had left he went up the back stairs into the kitchen and Mam told him that he had to go back to Chalfont on Monday morning. And this time he mustn't run away. If he did, both his Mam and Dad would be in serious trouble.

His mates told him she was only saying that so that he didn't go missing again, but he knew that he couldn't take the chance of getting his Mam into any more bother. At least he would see *King Kong* with his mates at the Empire.

~

Back at Chalfont Colony, Matron had been informed that Geordie had reached home safely and she told Sister Tate that he'd arrived back home to Newcastle on his own, in the early hours of the morning, safe and sound.

The following morning after breakfast, when Cockney was lining up for school, she told him that his friend would be back with them next Monday. As he opened his mouth to ask something, she stopped him short, telling him to be quiet and get in line. Cockney could tell that Sister Tate was relieved to let him know.

Cockney wanted to know whether Geordie had been picked up by the police, or whether he'd managed to get himself all that way up to the borders of Scotland on his own. That was one hell of a journey. Knowing his Geordie mate he wouldn't have much money in his pocket, if any. He would just have to wait and find out all about it when Geordie turned up.

~

In the streets and back lanes of Gateshead where Geordie lived it was the talk of the place. His mates said they could all have done it, they couldn't see what all the fuss was aboot. They all ended up going to see *King Kong*, including Geordie.

Monday morning soon came around. Before leaving for the station he told Mam that he would get a good hiding for going missing. Mam sat him down and told him face to face that if anyone laid a finger on him she would come down there and sort them out and take him home herself.

Geordie answered, 'You won't get to know Mam. They read our letters to home before they get sent.'

Mam could see he was uptight about going back after going missing from the bus. She gave him a hug and tried to reassure him that everything would be all right, 'Don't go worrying yourself son. I'll make sure that no one lays a finger on you, you hear me?'

'Yes Mam.'

He knew his Mam wouldn't tell him a lie and an hour later Geordie was once more standing at Central Station with his Mam, meeting up with Mr King.

'Well this is a rum do, isn't it?' Mr King said with a shake of his head.

Mam told Mr King that he had promised to behave himself and not to run away ever again.

Mr King knelt to look at him, face to face, 'If you run away George while I'm responsible for you, you'll get me the sack and then I'll be out of a job. You wouldn't want that to happen, would you George?'

Geordie looked at him and shook his head. Before getting on the train he gave his Mam a long hard hug around her waist, 'You won't forget to have me home for Christmas, will you Mam?'

'Don't you worry about that son. We'll see you at Christmas, I promise. I'll come and get you meself if I have to.'

Although he was pleased to hear that, he also knew Christmas was a long way off. This time he got on the train without being pulled away from Mam. Times like these always seemed the worst in his life. His Mam and where he lived were the only things he cared about. Everything outside of them meant nothing at all to him.

The train pulled out of Central Station as Geordie stood at the window, watching his Mam until she was no longer in sight. Mr King was very inquisitive about what Chalfont Colony looked like. Geordie wasn't in the mood to be talking about a place he didn't really like. But he knew his manners and told him a little bit about its large houses and small church hall; about the school that was opposite the homes for boys and girls up to the age of sixteen. Mr King asked him what happened when he turned sixteen? He told him he didn't know, because no one had ever told him. All he knew was that he had to stay at Tate House until he was sixteen.

This journey to Chalfont was slightly different. Mr King took him all the way to Tate House. From London, they travelled by train to Chalfont St Peter, where they got a taxi to the Colony. The taxi pulled up outside the main office building and Mr King was greeted by Matron. After a brief talk, Matron told the driver to take them to Tate House. When he pulled up outside the gardens of Sister Tate appeared at the front door. Geordie looked up at her and they said nothing for a few moments. Sister Tate invited Mr King inside and told George to go to the dining room to get a hot drink. After a while one of the attendants told George to follow him to the hall. Mr King was standing there and he asked Sister if he could have a word with George before leaving.

Mr King bent down to Geordie's level and said quietly, 'George, you really must try and settle down here. I mean, it looks a very nice place and, after all, your Mam and Dad have sent you for your own good. We can't have your Mam worrying about you all the time, can we now?'

'No sir,' he replied with a shake of his head.

'Right then George, so I'll look forward to seeing you at Christmas.'

George nodded as Sister Tate came out of her office.

'Time for supper young man, then off to bed with you. School in the morning.'

Mr King bid farewell as Geordie went to the dining room. While he was getting his supper Sister came in and stood in front of him with folded arms.

'Right young man. Do you realise the trouble you have caused everyone?'

He looked up at her, shaking his head, not saying a word.

'We'll talk in the morning before you go to school.'

After his supper he was told to brush his teeth and get to bed. As he walked into the dormitory the other kids stared at him, but not a soul spoke as he got changed into his pyjamas. The only one who was over the moon to see him was Cockney, who knew he had to talk to him before Sister Tate started questioning him the following morning – providing she hadn't done that already. After some time had passed, and hopefully everyone was asleep, Cockney threw his slipper at Geordie, who just turned over, still asleep. He threw his other slipper and hit Geordie smack on his head. That woke him up. He sat up, looking around to see who had hit his head.

'Geordie, it's me, Cockney,' he whispered.

'What? What you want? I was asleep,' he whispered back, keeping an eye open for the night duty officer sitting in his little room. Hopefully sleeping, as he usually did when not prowling around the beds, messing with some of the kids.

'Listen, Sister Tate thinks I helped you when you got off the bus. I've told her you weren't on the bus when I got on it. I saw you getting into the bin, that was brilliant. She stood next to the bin as well. Anyway, if she asks did you see me on the bus, tell her no you didn't, or else I'm in deep shit.'

'Yeah, right, okay. Noo git some sleep man.'

Just as Cockney was about to ask him how the hell had he managed to get back home, a voice came down the dormitory.

It was the night duty officer, 'The next person I hear talking will be in real trouble.'

~

The following morning after breakfast they were all lined up for school. Geordie included until Sister Tate pulled him out of the line and marched him into her office, which was larger than his Mam's kitchen.

'Right George. I only want to ask a few questions of you. Don't worry, you're not in any trouble if you tell me the truth.'

'Yes Sister,' he nodded.

'When you got off the bus did you walk out of the station with anyone?'

He shook his head, 'No Sister.'

'No one at all?'

'No Sister.'

'Did you walk out of the station the minute you got off the bus.'

He noticed that she was taking notes of his every answer.

'Did you walk out of the station as soon as you got off the bus?'

Again, he replied, 'No Sister.'

'Ah, so you went straight back down into Paddington underground station,' as if she had solved a mystery.

'No Sister. I waited until the bus had pulled away out of the station. Then I walked out of the station when it had gone, but I didn't know the streets in London like Newcastle and Gateshead, so I ended up getting lost.'

'George, are you telling me the truth? We looked everywhere on that station for you and you were nowhere to be found. Even the police couldn't find hide nor hair of you.'

He sat in front of her, not knowing what to say next.

'So, if you watched the bus pulling out of the station, where on earth were you watching from?'

'From the bin Sister.'

'Bin? What bin?' she asked.

'The bin behind the bus.'

'No, no, that's not possible. We searched high and low. We covered every square inch of that station and you were not in it.'

'Sister, I heard you talking to a policeman who told you that London was a dangerous place after dark, especially for children. And you told him I was some 300 miles from home.'

'So, tell me where you were hiding to hear this conversation?'

'I was in the rubbish bin at the back of the bus Sister.'

'Lord above! Who would ever have thought of such a place,' she sat back in her chair in astonishment.

'We always hide in the bins at home. One of my friends once hid under a bus and when it moved off he let go and fell on to the road. I was about to do that at the station when I got my eye on the rubbish bin.'

Sister Tate listened to how he finally managed to get back home from out of London up to Newcastle. After that she seemed to view Geordie in a different light. If he could do a journey like that with not a penny in his pocket, Chalfont to London would be a relatively simple journey for him. She knew that she would have to keep a close eye on him.

As George was leaving to go across the road to shool, she called out, 'Oh, just one last question George before you leave. Who were you sitting next to on the bus when you got off it?'

Geordie was too quick to be caught out like that, 'I don't think I was sitting with anyone Sister.'

'Oh, I thought you were sitting with your best friend. What's his name?'

'You mean the cockney lad?'

'Yes, that's right.'

'No. I didn't see him on the bus. I don't think anyone sat next to me Sister.'

'Hmm. Right, off to school with you then.'

She stood in the large front office window, watching him walk into the small school.

Geordie knocked on the headmaster's office door, who had a few words with him about behaving himself while at school then told him what class to report to. All eyes were on him as he entered the classroom.

Cockney could hardly wait to get outside on the field for their break. He wanted to know everything, 'I want to know how the fuck you managed to get back up to Newcastle', but first he needed to know had Sister Tate asked anything about Cockney knowing he was getting off the bus?

Geordie looked at his mate, 'Sorry pal, but I think I might have dropped you in it.'

Cockney's heart dropped, his face showed it all as he gave a moan, 'Agh, you fuckin didn't, did you?'

'Well, I never thought when she asked about seeing you on the bus and getting off it then seeing me climbing into the bin. Sorry Cockney, I didn't think.'

Cockney walked around in circles talking to himself, trying to get his head around what his mate had just told him, 'Now you've really fucked me up. My life's not going to be worth livin for the next few years, you fuckin prick.'

'Howled on. Or did I tell hor you weren't on the bus when I got off it, and hid in the bin?'

Cockney went silent as Geordie started to smile. Then he twigged. Geordie was pulling his leg. He wrapped his arm around his mate's neck and they wrestled with each other for a few moments. Geordie then told him everything that had happened, from going into London to getting home in the early hours of the morning.

'Tell you one thing,' said Cockney, 'I'll bet you any money she was saying a few Hail Marys when she got word you were back up in Newcastle on your own steam.'

Geordie couldn't understand what Cockney meant, so he simply let it go over the top of his head.

As time passed all thoughts of trying to get back home left him and he slowly adjusted to living in an institution. Sister Tate's attitude toward Geordie mellowed. Cockney often told him 'he'd get away with fuckin murder as far as she was concerned'.

While he was at Chalfont Colony, until he was sixteen, Geordie attended church every Sunday with everyone else, including harvest festivals. They were always big events that showed off all the fruit, veg and flowers grown by the older residents of the Colony.

Sister Tate sought permission for Geordie to attend confirmation lessons, and his parents gave their consent. He was confirmed by the Bishop of Buckinghamshire, which seemed to please Sister Tate no end. Personally, he couldn't see what all the fuss was about. He later told Cockney, 'You'd think she was talking to the King himself.'

When everyone at Tate House sat down in front of a fourteen-inch television set to watch the Coronation of Queen Elizabeth, I needn't say which two boys out of the 30-plus had the two best seats.

One of the things that Geordie never forgot was the time they were out on the field and he spotted what looked like an ambulance standing outside Tate House. He walked over and stood right next to the entrance. Two men in uniform came out, carrying a stretcher with a body on it, covered by a white sheet. It had to be one of the young lads, as the shape looked small to him. One of the other boys had also walked across to see what was going on, he told Geordie that it was young Hawthorn who had died in his sleep after taking a fit. Geordie asked him how'd he know that?

'Because I was only a couple of beds away from him when it happened.'

Sister Tate chased away the two of them – and the others who had started to come across from the field, 'Get back on the field. There's nothing here to see. Go on now.'

Geordie always wondered if he was the same boy he'd once encountered in the toilets, unable to get out of a constant fit but who knew someone was there even though he couldn't see who it was? The boy's name stayed with Geordie all his life because the sharp-thorned hedge all the way along the front of Tate House had the same name – it was a hawthorn hedge.

~

It did look to the mates as though Sister Tate had taken a shine to Geordie as he would get a ticking off, but if Cockney was in the same situation he'd get his ear clipped and be confined to bed.

Geordie was always going on about how they kept pigeons in the coalhouse back home. Cockney had no interest in pigeons whatsoever and when Geordie mentioned them he'd say, 'If you want pigeons mate, there's fuckin fousands of em in Trafalgar Square.'

One day Geordie mentioned he was wondering if Sister Tate would let him keep a few pigeons in the rear garden, which was mainly used for the kids to grow vegetables. Cockney laughed until the tears came to his eyes.

'You come up with some bright ones mate." Then, in an imitation of Sister Tate, he said, 'Oh, what a wonderful idea George. We could do with a bit of pigeon shite on the roofs. Now why didn't I think of that?'

Geordie shook his head and walked away over the field with his mate tagging along behind. Then he shouted, 'Makes no difference. I'm going to ask her anyway.'

'Yeah, of course you are. You do that mate. Why not?' Cockney shouted back as he rolled his eyes toward the sky, smiling at the very thought.

When Geordie finally got around to asking Sister if he could keep a couple of racing pigeons in the rear garden, away from the house, he was surprised to hear her say she would have to see someone about it first, but she would let him know.

Sister Tate was true to her word and soon told Geordie that he could keep two pigeons in the rear garden, but his parents would have to supply them.

He told Cockney that Sister had given him permission about the pigeons. Cockney's chin dropped to the ground in disbelief, 'Fuckin hell. What the hell's going on with you two?'

'She told me she would get one of the men residents to build a small place on legs to keep them in.'

'The next thing you'll be telling me is she wants to fuckin adopt you.'

Before long, a cardboard box arrived at Tate House. He took it out into the garden, and placed the two pigeons inside their small home. It was really a place built for rabbits, standing on four wooden legs, like the top end of his coalhouse back home. After over a week inside so they had a good look at where they were living, Geordie decided to see if they knew where they lived by letting one of them out. It sat on the roof of Tate House, not having a clue where it was supposed to go.

To try and coax it back into its small wooden home, he let the other one out the following day. But as much as he tried, he couldn't entice them back. The two pigeons stayed around for a week or two and eventually vanished, never to be seen again. But not before making a right old mess of the roof at the back end of the house with their poop. Although Sister didn't say anything to Geordie, you could tell she was not pleased about the mess they had left.

Although Geordie had noticed a pigeon loft in the garden of a bungalow at the entrance to the Colony, where the obelisk towered high into the sky, he'd never thought about asking if he could visit the loft, or that a guy with a proper pigeon loft might breed him two baby pigeons. It might have made him a better pigeon man. But it must be said that he did race pigeons with his Dad later in life, and did win many races out of France.

~

Life at Chalfont Colony rolled by at an awfully slow pace. Not a day went by when he didn't see someone on the ground taking a major fit. The weeks turned into months, and the months turned into years, with Geordie still taking his fits. The only feedback about them was from Cockney who, whenever he noticed any kind of change, would tell him about it.

He'd crack on to Geordie, trying to impersonate his accent, 'Whey aye man. It was hardly warth having that fit. Yi only tuck less than a minute. A wouldn't bother next time man.'

He was still taking at least one, sometimes two, a week. But the worst thing of all was when the sensations ran through his thighs and forearms and stopped him from getting to sleep at night. He couldn't control it or stop it happening. He never once saw Cockney take a fit, who only took them when he was asleep.

'Well, let's hope you don't end up getting carried out of here like young Hawthorn then,' Geordie told him.

'No way is that happening,' he replied. 'I'm out of here when I turn sixteen, even if I have to take to the streets of London. No way are they transferring me in with the rest of this lot. I've got a life to live.'

Geordie could tell that his Cockney mate meant every word, 'Yeah. And I'm with you.'

~

Geordie was just over fourteen when Cockney turned fifteen, still sweet on Shirley. Trouble was, the only time they could snatch together was at school as they changed lessons, which never lasted more than a jiffy. They depended on Shirley's mate Audrey and on Geordie to keep watch for them. They were desperate for a bit more time together, which was totally against all Colony rules and regulations.

Cockney approached his mate, 'Geordie would you do me a big favour?'

Knowing his mate well, Geordie was a bit apprehensive, 'Depends what it is.'

'Would you keep an eye open for me and Shirley?'

'What you on about? I do that already for you, you haven't got to ask us.'

'Nah, I don't mean at fuckin school.'

He didn't like the sound of that. He'd managed to keep out of trouble for quite a while and he knew the scrapes that his mate could get into and didn't want to be dragged into some hairballs scheme, 'Come on then. What is it?'

They walked into the middle of the field to make sure there were no other kids around before Cockney spoke, 'It's a big favour mind.'

'Yeah, and it's a big secret by the looks of it. Are you going to tell me what it is you want me to do or not?'

'Well, now we got moved to the small dormitory away from the night duty office, when the other four are asleep I could meet Shirley in the back garden. She's in a small dormitory, same as us, with her mate Audrey. But I need you to keep a watch out in case that night officer does his rounds. What do you say? Will you help us out mate?'

'And what happens if he decides to do one of his checks?'

'I've got a small torch, just flash it twice, close the window, and jump back into bed quick. You know what he's like, he only gives a quick glance at the beds.'

Geordie's bed was next to the window Cockney was on about. When he thought about it, it wasn't him that would be taking any chances, it was Cockney.

'Okay, but I'm only doing it once. It sounds too dodgy to me?'

'Aw, that's great mate. I'll tell Shirley tomorrow at school we'll do it Saturday night.'

Geordie knew that if they got caught the powers that be would kick the two of them out as far as they could possibly kick them. The last thing he wanted was to get his Mam into any bother, after keeping his nose clean all this time.

There was no doubt he was now institutionalised, as once upon a time he would have said yes without thinking about it.

CHAPTER 9

O N THE FRIDAY before the Saturday set up for
Cockney and Shirley, they were sitting at their
school desks and Geordie didn't feel well. He knew
what was happening with the sensations he was having.

His teacher, the only male teacher the school had, could
see that Geordie was starting to fidget about in his seat, as
he had in the past before a fit. The teacher stopped what he
was doing and got Geordie out of his desk and stood him in
front of him. Cockney watched the teacher's every move as
he clasped both hands on his mate's face, and placed his face
right up to Geordie's, with their noses practically touching.
At first Cockney, thought he was going to kiss Geordie.

The whole class heard every word as the teacher said,
'George. Look deep into my eyes. You are not going to take
this fit. Do you hear what I am telling you? You will not take
this fit. Do you understand me?'

The teacher kept on repeating his words at Geordie with
their noses touching. Then Geordie fell to the floor and had
a fit.

At dinner time Geordie asked Cockney what had
happened in the class. All he could remember was the teacher
holding his face with the palms of his hands and talking to
him.

'What was he saying?'

'He was telling you not to take a fit.'

'Then what happened?'

'What do you think? You took your fit and then you came round, like you always do, as if nothing had happened.'

'What was that all about I wonder?' asked Geordie.

'Well, if you're asking me, I'd say it looked like he was trying to hypnotise you into not taking a fit.'

'I tried to fight it, but it didn't make any difference, I still conked out, didn't I?'

That was the one and only time the teacher ever tried that with him.

~

Saturday night came round and Cockney kept reminding his mate about keeping watch for him and Shirley. As Geordie climbed into bed, he thought it was just as well there were only six beds in that dormitory, as no way would he have agreed to it if they'd been in one of the bigger dormitories with too many prying eyes. Before he knew it he was fast asleep, until something hit him on the head. It was Cockney's slipper.

Cockney had puffed up the blankets on his bed to make it look as if he was in it, 'Come on, get out of bed and give us a hand to lift this window.'

It was pitch black outside, there were no stars only clouds. With a struggle they lifted the bottom sash of the large old wooden window. Cockney handed his mate a small torch as he climbed out and dropped a few feet into the garden. He looked up at Geordie, 'Now you know what to do, don't you?'

'Yeah, yeah. If I see anyone, I give you a quick flash with the torch.'

Cockney walked across to the hedge that separated the two gardens. To his delight Shirley was waiting for him. Geordie could just about make them out in the darkness, but he soon started to get a bit on edge, what with the window open and them two playing lovey dovey where anyone might see them. He'd had enough and gave the little torch a couple of flashes, only to hear Cockney whisper loudly, 'Turn that fuckin torch off you idiot.'

'Get yourself back in here quick.'

After a last, long kiss Cockney came hurrying back and scrambled up into the dormitory. They quickly closed the window. Before long, the two of them were fast asleep in bed.

The following morning Cockney said to Geordie, 'I could have had another ten minutes with her if you hadn't flashed that fuckin torch you idiot.'

'Yeah, and you could have been seen, or even caught in the act if I hadn't flashed it, you fucking idiot,' he replied.

Cockney knew he was in the wrong as he mumbled, 'Aw well, I suppose.'

~

Sister was keen that Geordie become a Scout. Meetings were once a week in the church hall, but all he remembered was having to learn the Scout mottoes, parrot fashion, 'Trusty-Loyal-Helpful-Brotherly-Courteous-Kind-Obedience-Smile-Thrifty. Clean in Body and Mind.' He later read that they used to go camping and did various other activities but he couldn't recall anything he did as a scout at Chalfont Colony, from thirteen to sixteen years old.

Sister also decided that he should learn Irish dancing. Maybe because both Ireland and Scotland had special ways of dancing and she felt he was from close to the Scottish border and that his accent seemed to warrant it. What Sister soon discovered was that the Geordie boy from Gateshead had two left feet. She soon gave up on that project.

~

Cockney told Geordie that now he was sixteen he would be leaving Chalfont Colony for good at Christmas, which was looming ever closer. When Christmas did come around, Geordie was pleased to be going home, but was a bit downhearted that when they were over, he wouldn't have the company of his mate Cockney, who he'd spent the last four plus years with, both day and night.

Those going home for Christmas climbed aboard the bus standing outside Tate House. The two of them sat together, with Cockney next to the window, having a long last look at Tate House, where he had spent the last six and a half years. As the bus went through the entrance gates Geordie looked at him. He sensed that Cockney felt some kind of sadness as he looked at Tate House field until it was no longer in sight.

'Do you think you'll miss the place?' Geordie asked.

'No fuckin way mate.'

'What are you going to do about getting a job? I take it you will want to work, don't you?'

'Aw, I'll get a job okay. Even if I go on the market runs with my uncle Sid.'

There was a slight pause then Cockney turned to his mate, 'Listen Geordie, whatever you do, when it's your turn and you turn sixteen, we're only talking about six months, don't let them try and convince you to stay on a bit longer, to move you into another house with older people. You fuckin leave.'

'Yeah but where?' Geordie thought, Gateshead isn't as big and busy as London. 'Hmm,' was all Cockney heard.

'If you can get back up to Newcastle with not a penny in your pocket, you'll be okay. Take my word for it mate.'

'Well, I did have a half a crown off me Dad.'

'Yeah well, you know what I mean?'

'Suppose so,' replied Geordie.

Before they knew it, the bus pulled into Paddington Station and everyone stood up all excited, until a sharp voice came over the top of all the chatter.

'SIT DOWN EVERYONE. NOW.'

The whole bus went silent immediately. Cockney was still standing as he looked down at Geordie, smiling, 'And you ask me will I miss this place.'

Sister called out the name of each boy and duly handed each one over to their parent or guardian. Cockney's name was called out before Geordie's and he was off the bus before him. By the time his name was called, and Sister had handed him over to Mr King, Cockney was nowhere in sight, with the place being crowded and busy.

'Nice to see you again George. You ready for your Christmas holidays then?'

Nodding, Geordie replied that he was. He paused before getting on the escalator for a last look toward the station exit and there was Cockney with his mum, waving his arms all over the place. He waved back as Cockney showed his two thumbs in the air. Geordie put down his small suitcase and did the same thing with his thumbs back to Cockney.

That was the last time they saw each other.

~

When Geordie first came home he felt a bit like a stranger, with his southern-type accent. Also, he wasn't as wild and rowdy as the other kids, some of them even smoked.

The council had given Mam and Dad a new-built council house with three bedrooms, a sitting/dining room, a separate kitchen and an inside toilet and bathroom, with hot and cold water. They still had the coal fire for heating as there was no central heating then.

Although they now had three bedrooms, he still had to bunk in with his other three brothers in one bed, and the bedroom could only take a three-quarter size bed. Someone had to sleep at the bottom end, but Mam always made sure that it wasn't to be Geordie. It was always a bit strange climbing into bed with his three brothers. But it was heaven sleeping in T-shirt and underpants instead of pyjamas. On top of everything else, he had got that used to saying his prayers every night before bed that he would say them in bed to himself.

The fits were still with him. He was no longer taking them every other day, but he was taking at least one if not two a week. He did his best to keep out of sight whenever he felt one coming on. By now, most of his old mates were working, which made him feel a bit out of place when he saw any of them. His not much older sister had started working and it wouldn't be long before his brothers would be following her down that road. Whenever anyone asked him where he was working, he would reply that he hadn't found a job yet.

Geordie would be sixteen in the May after the Christmas holidays. He was beginning to wonder if staying on at Chalfont Colony might be the best thing to do, knowing that it would be difficult to get a job. He had prayed to God for over five years, gone to church every Sunday morning, and even been confirmed by a Bishop. Now he was praying to God to help him as his mind was all mixed up. He could stay on at Chalfont Colony where he didn't feel out of place any longer, or leave Chalfont and take his chances up on Tyneside with its streets and dirty back lanes. Totally the opposite to what he had become accustomed to.

He kept wondering if Cockney would get a job or not. He knew the moment you told any prospective employer that you took fits, and that you'd been in an institution for epileptics for the past six years, your chances of getting any kind of job would drop to practically zero. In the mid-1950s epilepsy still carried a stigma. He also thought that if Cockney took his fits when he was asleep and didn't tell his prospective employer where he had been over the past seven years he would stand a good chance of getting decent employment. But Geordie's situation was totally different, and he knew it, nevertheless the pull of wanting to leave Chalfont was strong in him, especially now that Cockney wouldn't be coming back.

There was only him and his Mam in the house when he came out and asked the question he hadn't asked for over three years, 'Mam, how much longer do I have to go to Chalfont Colony? Or am I never going to leave?'

Mam was a bit taken aback at first, 'Don't be daft man. No, you're not going there forever. What makes you think that like?'

'I'm sixteen in five months, then I've got to leave Tate House and go into another one with people older than me. I've had enough Mam, it's been over five years and I don't want to be placed into another house with older people. I want to stay at home Mam, I really do. If you'll have me.'

Mam could see he was really upset. She went across to the settee and placed her arm around his shoulders, 'It's alreet son, divint worry. I'll tark ti your Dad aboot it when he gets in from work, alreet?'

Geordie did not answer for a few moments, then said, 'If I have to go back after I'm sixteen they will put me into one of the grown-up homes. If that happens Mam, I don't want to come home for holidays anymore, like some kid still at school.'

Mam was shocked, 'Why ever not pet? I mean, you love coming home.'

'I just feel out of place every time I come back. Honestly Mam, I don't know where I belang anymore.'

Mam gave him another hug and told him she would speak to his Dad about it when he got in from work and not to start worrying. She would sort it one way or another. Geordie nodded, got up and walked out the back door.

Dad came home from working the late shift at the pit and after he'd had his bath, Mam told him what Geordie had said to her about not wanting to come home anymore, and him not knowing where he belonged anymore. She asked him what he thought about it all. He didn't answer. He sat down in his armchair next to the open coal fire. Mam brought him his dinner, then a mug of tea. He kept on eating his dinner

Finally, without looking up, Dad said, 'Aye well, in that case I think he's been there lang enough. It's time he was yem, before yi lose him for good woman. Aye, ye tell him, when he torns sixteen he comes yem for good. Alreet?'

'Aye, I'll tell him,' Mam answered with a lighter heart.

'Yi di nah he'll have a hell of a job trying to get any kind of work, divint yi?'

'We'll deal with that when it comes a lang,' Mam answered.

When Mam told Geordie what his Dad had said he felt like crying. As his eyes started to water, he said, 'Thanks Mam,' and walked out the door so she couldn't see his tears. That was one of the best Christmas presents he'd ever had.

After the holidays were over Mam told him as he boarded the train once more for King's Cross, 'This is the last time son, alreet?'

He gave his Mam a hug, 'Yeah Mam. Love you.'

Mam called out, pointing at him with her finger and smiling, 'And behave yourself, you hear me?'

CHAPTER 10

BACK AT CHALFONT Colony he changed into his khaki shirt and short trousers once again. For the first time he felt stupid standing in short trousers.

He didn't know if Sister Tate had been informed that he would be leaving Chalfont after May. Sister didn't make much comment, 'Hmm, we'll see about that later.'

He didn't follow what she'd meant but gave it no more thought. If his Dad said he had been there long enough, then that was good enough for him.

Geordie turned sixteen on the thirteenth of May 1955. Sister Tate had a cake made for him and all the boys at Tate House sang 'Happy Birthday'. He'd never known anyone else having a cake made. It was usually only a song, or else they'd have to make birthday cakes every other day. This got Geordie thinking about Cockney, and what he'd said about being Sister's favourite.

Geordie had a small calendar and started crossing off the months to leave, then it went from months to weeks, until finally he was counting the number of days that were left. As he lay in bed the night before he was due to leave Chalfont for the last time his mind ran over the things that had happened during his years at Tate House.

Sister Tate had done her utmost to help him settle into the way life was at Chalfont Colony. Even more so after the day he went back home on his own from London to Newcastle on Tyne. It may have been that she had understood his background, he didn't really know, but one thing he did know was, she had done her best for him. Even to the point of allowing pigeons to be sent down from Newcastle and having a place built for them in the rear garden – and she'd never once complained to Geordie about the right old mess on the roof or their disappearance, which in itself was unusual. From when he first arrived at Tate House until the day he left, he had to admit to himself that not one person had ever mistreated him in any way.

The following morning the bus pulled up outside of Tate House and, as usual, the kids going home for the summer were jumping with excitement as they watched the bus from the dining room windows. They hurried outside, and he was left standing on his own in the dining room, he gave it one last look before closing the door behind him.

He sat on the back seat of the bus, looking out the rear window, watching the few kids standing on the edge of the field where he had spent his teen years. There was the solitary tree which he had attempted to climb many times but failed, it didn't seem as big as when he'd seen it for the first time all those years ago. He looked at the kids standing there like zombies, not one of them talking to each other. These were the kids who were not going home for the summer holidays. Every one of their sad faces had a story to tell. He knew that every single one of their hearts were breaking, thinking that their Mam or Dad didn't want them. He asked himself how any parent wouldn't put themselves out for their kids?

Sister Tate did her usual name count before allowing the driver to pull away. When she called out Geordie's name, he slid down his seat, not answering. She called it out for the second time and took a few steps down the bus, 'I know you're there George, so please answer when I call out your name.'

He stood up and called out with a smile, 'Present Sister.'

'I should think so to,' as she smiled back at him.

As the bus pulled away, he gave a last look at Tate House, wondering if he would ever see it again.

The bus pulled into Paddington Station, where the crowds of parents and guardians had been waiting patiently for their arrival. Geordie waited for his name to be called out by Sister Tate. It looked as though he was going to be one of the last names called, or possibly the last. Finally, Sister called out his name and he stepped down off the bus, where Mr King greeted him with a smile and put h'is signature to Sister's form.

She looked at Geordie and, in her strong Irish accent, said, 'Well here we are then George. This is where your life begins. You take good care of yourself, you hear me? You'll do all right for yourself, of that I'm sure. Now off with you and break someone else's heart.'

Geordie was surprised when she placed her arm around him and hugged him toward herself for one brief second. In all the time he had been at Chalfont he had never seen her give anyone a hug. She then turned her attention toward Mr King, shook his hand, told him it had been a pleasure knowing him and, with a smile, to 'keep his eye on this boy as he has a tendency to wander off and go home on his own.'

Mr King smiled back, 'I will Sister. And it's been my pleasure.'

With that said, the two of them turned and walked toward the underground, at the top of the escalator Geordie turned for a last look across to where the bus was standing. Sister Tate was on the steps of the bus looking out across the station. He raised his arm and waved, not expecting her to notice him, but to his surprise she gave him a wave.

'Come along George, we have to catch the train at King's Cross,' Mr King told him. They disappeared down into the underground.

Once they were on the train at King's Cross Station and settled into their seats, they were soon speeding toward Newcastle and home. The journey gave him plenty of time to reflect on what was ahead of him and his years spent at Chalfont Colony.

He had to admit that neither Chalfont Colony nor Sister Tate had done him any harm.

Yes, he had hated the place for the first year and a half, possibly due to it being an entirely different environment to what he'd been accustomed to.

Yes, it was a boring life, leastways for him.

Yes, life was completely different to the back lanes and cobbled streets he had known.

Yes, it was a very regimented way of life.

Yes, he was taught manners.

Yes, he was taught to respect authority.

Yes, he was taught to respect his elders.

Yes, he had been confirmed Church of England.

Yes, going to church every Sunday and all the ceremonies that went with it had brought him closer to God.

Yes, he had lost most of his Geordie accent at Chalfont.

Yes, his medications were given night and day at a precise time.

Yes, you went to bed at the same time every night.

Yes, you were up at the same time every morning, doing the same regular routine.

Yes, the silence screamed at you at times.

Never at any time did you have reason to get excited.

The only time Geordie could remember was the Queen's Coronation, when the television set was hired so the boys could watch it live. It was the first time any of them had seen a television set. Unfortunately, the pleasure was short-lived as the set went back after a couple of days.

Did all or any of this cure him of his epilepsy? No, his seizures continued well into adulthood. The only difference was a slight drop in the number that he was having after he left Chalfont Colony.

~

It was a good feeling to be back home once again and not having to keep thinking about how long before he had to return to Chalfont.

A couple of his Mam's old neighbours had moved about the same time and into the same street when they received their new council houses from Gateshead Council. They sat talking about him as if he wasn't standing there in Mam's sitting room with them, commenting on how politely he spoke and acted.

'Eh, eh doesn't tark like us does he Gorty?'

'I wouldn't worry about that,' Mam answered. 'He'll be back to his old self, given time.'

Mam was more concerned about him taking any seizures when she wasn't there for him. He was on the same medication as when he had first started taking his seizures – 60mg of phenobarbital each morning, 100mg of Epanutin (a phenytoin) morning and night. It was slightly different now that he was no longer a small kid playing in the back lanes. Had they done the right thing taking him out of an environment where they knew he was safe? All she could do was try her best to keep an eye on him, but that was going to be difficult.

Geordie had been home from Chalfont Colony for three months, doing his best to try and find a job but to no avail. Every time he mentioned he was an epileptic the interview was cut short. No one wanted to take the risk of anything happening to him while he was working for them. He was shunned by everyone who interviewed him. Even the unemployment services failed to find him work as a lowly labourer.

It was 1955 and he soon found out for himself there was a stigma toward epileptics. All the excuses in the world came from people who seemed prepared to take him on, until he mentioned the word fits. There were times after an interview, when he would think of Sister Tate telling him he would do all right for himself. If she could only see him now, she'd probably take it all back.

He was sitting on the settee with his Dad reading the newspaper on a Thursday just after dinner time when Mam came in with her shopping, which she put down in the kitchen. She came into the sitting room and sat herself down facing the two of them and then announced that she had got Geordie an interview for a job the following morning. He didn't get too excited about it, he'd been at that stage of the game quite a few times.

It was Dad who asked, 'An interview doing what?'

'It's an interview for Charlie Young's.'

'Charlie Young, who the hell's Charlie Young when he's at yem?' Dad asked.

'Aw, it's not delivering papers is it Mam?' cried Geordie.

'No, don't be daft,' she replied.

'Well, are you going to tell us or keep it a secret?' asked Dad.

'It's an interview for Charlie Young's shop on Sunderland Road.'

'So, what is it? Is it a grocer, a butcher or a candlestick maker? Come on then woman, are yi going ti tell us or not?' cried Dad, getting impatient.

Geordie just sat and listened to the two of them. Mam glanced across at Dad, then turned her gaze on Geordie and said in a low voice, 'It's Charlie Young's the butcher's shop.'

Dad looked at her as if she was out of her mind.

'A butcher's shop! Are yee oot of ya tiny mind or what? He'd be safer working doon the pit than deeing that, yi frigging idiot,' shouted Dad, who couldn't believe what he was hearing.

'Well, it's as good as anything he's going ti get,' she replied sharply.

'Agh, wye aye, nice razor-sharp knives that can cut ya fingers off nee bother in one slice. It's just the frigging job he wants, yi idiot.'

'Well it's better than him sitting here al day lang,' she replied.

'Aw aye, it couldn't have been a fruit shop, or a grocer's, awe nar, that would have been too easy for him wouldn't it? A frigging butcher's shop.'

'I wouldn't worry Dad,' Geordie replied with a little laugh, 'I probably won't get it anyway. It'll be like the other interviews.'

'Huh knowing wor luck you'll end up gitting it,' he rattled his newspaper and tried to get back to reading it.

The following morning the Geordie and his Mam took the short walk, down the bankside field outside their door, to Sunderland Road, where a small number of shops were clustered together, away from the main Gateshead High Street, surrounded by dozens of long terraces of houses.

On their way to the interview Mam told him that the manager of the shop, Mr Knox, knew all about him taking his bad turns, as Mam used to put it. She told him to speak politely, with no slang words, 'Just think you are answering the way people at Chalfont Colony would have expected you to answer them. And above all, be polite, and don't forget to tell him that you know when you're going to have a bad turn.'

He could see the shop from across the other side of the road as they approached it, he saw the sign in the window saying BOY WANTED. Mam waited until there were no customers in the shop before walking in with Geordie. They waited for the manager.

'This is my laddie.'

'I'll take him into the back where my office is if you don't mind. We can talk in private. We shouldn't be long, all right?'

Mam told him she needed to get a few groceries and would come back after they'd finished. They entered a small office where they sat at a desk.

The manager said his mam had told him that he had been down south in a special home for people who took fits. The first question he asked was, when he took one of his fits did he know what had happened when he came out of it? And how long was his fit, time wise?

After about half an hour they came out of the office and Mam was waiting for them.

'I'll speak to the area manager on Saturday when he comes in. If you call in this time next week I'll have an answer for you. Sorry I can't do it any sooner, he's a busy man with another five shops to see to. I'll try my best for him though.'

Mam thanked him and Geordie turned looked at the manager saying, in a very polite manner, 'Thank you very much sir.'

The manager replied, 'That's all right son.'

On the way home, Mam was eager to know what the conversation was all about. He told her everything that the manager had asked, and how he had replied. Mam told him she had a good feeling about it, 'but let's keep our fingers and toes crossed.' She asked him what he thought about working there, and did he think he'd like it if he did get it?

'Yeah I'd work anywhere Mam,' he told her.

Although he was optimistic about getting the job, he didn't tell Mam that, and after a few days he soon forgot all about it. The following Saturday morning Mam reminded him that they had to go and see the manager at Charlie Young's at five o'clock. Mam made him put on his Sunday best, commenting on how smart he looked. He got the impression that Mam was more nervous than he was. The manager smiled when he saw the two of them standing waiting to see him.

'Well pet, I've spoken to the area manager who has told me that he's willing to give your laddie a month's trial to see how he gets on. But only on condition that if anything happens to him when he takes one of his fits you won't hold us responsible for it – as you said before. It's up to you pet. What do you think?'

Mam was over the moon. She thanked the manager and agreed once again to the condition.

'In that case George, you can start on Monday morning at eight o'clock. Wear something casual, you don't want good clothes smelling of meat, do you?' He smiled down at Geordie, who smiled back. 'Oh, and don't forget, he'll need to bring his P45 with him.'

Mam was walking on air all the way home. Geordie couldn't believe it, he had a job, and all down to his Mam, who wouldn't be beaten where her laddie was concerned. He asked her what he'd meant about needing his P45.

'It's something you hand in to whoever employs you. Don't worry pet, I'll sort that out for you. It's in the house.'

Dad wasn't sure it was the right kind of job for him, but he didn't put the damper on his lad getting it. He told him to be extra careful where knives were concerned, as they would be as sharp as razor blades. Mam told him his Dad was right, and if he didn't feel well at any time to make sure that he put a knife down if he was holding one.

Monday morning came and Geordie was up early, not wanting to be late on his first day. Mam told him she had to go to the shops so she would go down that way with him. He knew she wanted to go with him so he didn't say anything. The shop directly faced his old school, where some of the kids were already starting to go in.

As he looked at the kids it brought back memories, then he turned his gaze across the road at the butcher's shop. It had been there when he was at school but he had never given it a second thought. It was more than likely he'd see some of his old teachers, or even his old headmaster, Mr May.

'What is it?' Mam always knew when something was worrying him or putting him on edge. 'Are you all right?'

'Yeah, I'm all right Mam. But I'd like to go in on my own. Would you mind?'

'No if that's what yi want son. Go on, get yourself across, like I've told you. Just be careful what you're doing, alreet?'

He crossed the road, giving his Mam who stood watching him from the kerbside a quick glance before he took his first step into Charlie Young's butcher shop. And the first steps into a working life.

Little did Geordie know what life had in store for him. He was going on to do things that no epileptic in those years would ever have dreamt of doing.

But that, my friend, is another story.

Lightning Source UK Ltd.
Milton Keynes UK
UKHW012006180621
385770UK00003B/841